Joe & Andrea,

Thank you for your continued friendship and belief in me. I praise God for crossing our paths. May He always be your source.

[signature]

4/28/21

What people are saying about...

Practical Leadership: Lessons from an Average Leader

"This is a must-read, not only for those privileged to already be in leadership positions, but for anyone who is committed to being a leader in their own lives. Gregg does an incredible job sharing stories from his career and explaining critical leadership lessons that will help you in your own pursuit. He exemplifies servant leadership and provides countless examples of how he has effectively led others, whether it be on the battlefield or in the classroom. Trust me, Gregg is anything but average, and his insights will serve as valuable lessons and reminders to each reader as they continue to hone their leadership skills."

Allison Kreiger Walsh
VP of Advanced Recovery Systems
Founder, Allison Walsh Enterprises, LLC

"Dr Mays breaks leadership down to its bare essentials. He lays himself bare to the benefit of everyone that takes this leadership journey with him. This book is a must read whether you are just starting out on your leadership journey or you are trying to add more tools to your tool kit."

Jim Hewitt
Colonel, US Air Force

"Gregg lives his life strongly exemplifying his unshaken faith in God, to know Gregg is to know God. His dynamic personality, strong leadership abilities and his passion for the love of God are all a huge part of who he is and what you will witness while in his presence. Being a practical leader comes natural for Gregg, the experiences he shares in this book are extreme measures that will sharpen your high character, integrity, and moral courage."

Keith Williams
Chairman of the Board
Miss Florida Scholarship Program

"A timely read! In today's business environment we are faced with rapid changes, new technologies, and uncertainty driven by customers' expectations for better, faster, cheaper products and services. As companies push to reinvent with pace, leaders are expected to do the same. This book truly brought me back to the basics of leadership and more importantly a reminder to be an authentic leader. The story-telling approach in the book kept my interest and made me want more. The lesson's learned and shared by Coach Mays contain great wisdom and an authentic experience which provide great take a-ways that transcend across any leadership role whether in business, leading a classroom, volunteering, etc. I recommend this book for all leaders that need to take the time to reset and get back to both leadership basics and genuine self-reflection."

John Monsanto
Claims Manager
State Farm

"Gregg Mays is one of the most inspirational mentors I have met in my own life, so when I heard he was writing a book on leadership I could not wait to read it. *Practical Leadership: Lessons from an Average Leader* features relatable and inspiring perspectives that draws you in while simultaneously allowing you take a step back to reflect. I was captivated by each story and uplifted by the many lessons that I learned from Gregg's own experience. After reading this book, I can confidently say that I approach leadership in a new light and would recommend it to anyone who wants to become a better leader."

Emily English
Student
Northeastern University

PRACTICAL LEADERSHIP: LESSONS FROM AN AVERAGE LEADER

FOUR ATTRIBUTES ALL EFFECTIVE LEADERS POSSESS

DR. GREGG MAYS

Practical Leadership: Lessons from an Average Leader
© 2021 by Gregg Mays. All rights reserved.

Published by Author Academy Elite
PO Box 43, Powell, OH 43065
www.AuthorAcademyElite.com

Identifiers:
LCCN: 2021901483
ISBN: 978-1-64746-693-0 (paperback)
ISBN: 978-1-64746-694-7 (hardback)
ISBN: 978-1-64746-695-4 (ebook)

Available in paperback, hardback, e-book, and audiobook

All Scripture quotations, unless otherwise indicated, are taken from
the Holy Bible, New International Version®, NIV®. Copyright © 1973,
1978, 1984 by Biblica, Inc.™ Used by permission. All rights reserved
worldwide.

Any Internet addresses (websites, blogs, etc.) and telephone numbers
printed in this book are offered as a resource. They are not intended in
any way to be or imply an endorsement by Author Academy Elite, nor
does Author Academy Elite vouch for the content of these sites and
numbers for the life of this book.

Some names and identifying details have been changed to protect the
privacy of individuals.

I dedicate this book to Son Hui Mays and Candice Mays (aka Michele Jang). Your support is felt and appreciated. I love you both.

In memory of Juanita Mays, my mother, who put the desire to write a book inside me when I was a young boy. I miss you daily.

TABLE OF CONTENTS

Leaders Must—Create a Positive Leadership Climate

Leaders Must—Communicate Effectively

Leaders Must—Be Humble

Leaders Must— Persevere

FOREWORD

By V. R. Vogt

Highly respected and cherished by all who know him, Dr. Gregg Mays has masterfully crafted a novel way of reaching a reader's interest! Describing the lessons and examples learned when being in leadership positions himself over the years, his technique of writing not only entices the reader to want to read more, but I have found it had me ruminating on my own roles in life when reading *Practical Leadership: Lessons from an Average Leader*.

When I was first approached by Dr. Mays, asking me if I would mind reading his book prior to publishing, I would have never thought such a topic would intrigue me. Turns out, it did! It not only held my interest, but it actually captivated me because there are parts that had me reflecting on my past mistakes when I was in a leadership position running a non-profit organization. Back before I published my *Tempted Knights* series, I worked as a volunteer running a non-profit organization for military families on three different occasions, at three locations over a span of nearly seven years. Had I read this book years ago, I could have, would have, and yes, should have done things much differently and avoided those mistakes I had made.

Back when I was in those leadership positions, I probably read something like a dozen or more self-help kind of leadership books out on the market. Let me say the one word that comes to mind when thinking of those other books—*boring*! Unlike others I have read, Dr. Mays uses a unique approach to help the reader fully absorb the lessons he shares, which includes openly putting out there his own personal stories with humility, description, clarification, and even a bit of humor at the appropriate time. He gives the reader real useful tools to put into action for those who could use them.

Perhaps you have considered reading this book to assist you in the position you are in, be it for your career, volunteer work, or perhaps you are a teacher or in a leadership position on a team of some kind. Heck, maybe you are a single parent running a full household and simply looking for a little direction to help you stay in charge of your house. No matter the occupation or title, this book could be very beneficial for all because, in my opinion, *Practical Leadership: Lessons from an Average Leader* covers all the important bases for all different types of leadership in this world. Everything from building a positive work environment relationship, trust, and respect of those under you, to good or bad decision-making, which includes areas like problems that can easily happen as well as be avoided where situations may arise, *e.g.*, the proper way of critiquing those under your leadership, such as when and how criticism can help or hurt those under you. Dr. Mays masterfully covers important lessons and enlightens the reader how certain approaches of communication can either help or even jeopardize your leadership position itself.

I was very impressed when reading this book because while Dr. Mays writes mostly about his leadership experiences and examples from his time while in service in our armed forces, the text in *Practical Leadership: Lessons from an Average Leader* is written in a smooth flowing style. Furthermore, although I am a military spouse, as a civilian who lacks a great deal of knowledge when it comes to what I call "military lingo" and their terms, I appreciate how Dr. Mays uses simple definitions for things like military acronyms, words, terms, and so on, which makes the entire book easy for non-military to understand. That also makes many of the stories he shares with the reader come across as relatable in many circumstances.

You will not be bored or bogged down with complicated words like one of those typical "step-by-step" "how-to" become a leader books out there on the market. Rather, this book gave me detailed insight from an experienced individual—one who knows all too well about how easy it is to make a mistake in the moment when simple things like emotions get the better of us.

Yes, Dr. Mays helps the reader understand and become aware of moments such as that, including preventative measures one could take to help avoid them. He mentions certain methods he had learned over the years to better manage stressful and unavoidable situations that often arise while in a leadership position. This is where I could have used his advice and guidance when it came to me better handling stressful moments while being in charge of those non-profit organizations for military families. Having volunteers working under me was not always easy when one of them would try to start rumors among the other volunteers to stir up some drama. Whether she was jealous of the other women or had a mean streak in her, I am not sure. I was very upset—angry. We were all volunteers there to help people, not break people down. After reading this book and looking back now, I realize I should have talked to her alone to find out why she had been trying to start trouble among the other volunteers instead of calling her out in front of them. My actions done in the heated moment of emotions caused the rumor-spreading individual to stop volunteering altogether. Volunteers are not paid. They are there to help support the soldiers and their families. Losing even one volunteer was a great loss for the organization.

Dr. Mays goes over similar situations like the one I was faced with, which is how I found myself looking back at my other mistakes I have made in those leadership positions as a volunteer, in addition to even now as an author with people working under me.

Therefore, I highly recommend this *Practical Leadership: Lessons from an Average Leader* to everyone from young adult to old. I truly believe this is one book that would be beneficial to all who read it. To be completely honest, the only complaint I have regarding this book is that it was not written years ago for me to read and help me in my own leadership role. Nevertheless, I am very glad to have read it now!

ACKNOWLEDGMENTS

It has been said before, and it must be said here, an undertaking like this is not done without a team effort. Therefore, I must take this time to acknowledge those who have helped me with this book project.

The first thank you goes to God. Without His influence in my life, no way I could persevere through the two-plus years it took to write this book and see it through to publication. One of the biggest influences He had on my life was allowing me to find my wife, Son Hui, who has been a major supporter every step of the way. I would be crazy not to acknowledge her right after God. Our daughter, Michele, is right next to my wife with her support of this endeavor. If you are a parent, then you know there are few things sweeter to hear than your child saying, "I'm proud of you." Thank you, Michele, for saying those words to me.

The support of family and friends and the belief all had in my ability to write this book spurred me forward on the days when I would have rather watched more tv or do anything else except write. Many of you willingly took your time to read chapters and provide feedback. It is what enabled me to finish. Your comments were useful to help me write something that will be helpful to all who read it.

I am thankful for Jessica Maldonado and Laura Baldwin. Jessica is responsible for all of the graphic design at the end of this book. She is a professional. Laura did the initial edit of this book. She took a poorly constructed book with a good idea and turned it into something that people would want to read. Her tireless efforts are appreciated.

Other big thanks go out to everyone who financially supported the publication of this book. Without your belief in this project, those who read it and gain from it may have never had the opportunity to grow as a leader. I cannot say thank you enough. I pray that you receive blessings 100-fold of what you gave.

I want to give special thanks to Matt and Makenzie Braly. Their generous donation had a major impact on the confidence I need to sit down and pen the next book in the *Practical Leadership* series. Matt, your words were powerful. I was overwhelmed when you said, "This is not charity; I believe in you." I cannot say thank you enough for your belief. I also thank you for the many book recommendations through the years. I pray that this book is up to the standard you have for yourself.

I would like to thank three couples who have believed in me from the first time we met. Thank you, Jules and Kathy Massee, Joe and Andrea Bowen, and Mike and Tanya Reeves. Your generous gifts are appreciated. But more importantly, your continued support of all I do has lifted me in times of need. Thank you.

My final thanks go to you, the reader. There are millions of books, but you chose to read this one. That blows my mind. It is not lost on me. Thank you for using this book as a part of your leadership journey. I pray that the lessons within will improve you as a leader and inspire you to be an exceptional leader. Enjoy the book! I would also appreciate your feedback as I sit down to pen the next book in the *Practical Leadership: Lessons From an Average . . .* series.

INTRODUCTION

Who is Gregg Mays, and why should you read his book? That is a good question. The answer to the first question is Gregg Mays is an average leader who has been able to reach about every goal he has set for himself. I have done this by maintaining an unshakable faith in God. This faith has allowed me to accept the things I cannot change and go full force after those things that I can change. I have learned through the years that leadership takes on many forms. How you lead is based on who you are as much as whom you are leading. I have learned that leadership is an art as much as it is a science. There are certain things in leadership that work, no matter what; it is the science of leadership. To be a good leader, you must have high character, integrity, and moral courage. No matter whom you are leading, these are must traits. However, I have learned that each group of people you lead have different needs and triggers to excellence. That is where the "art" of leadership comes in. You must work on the art of leadership every day; therefore, reading books and attending leadership conferences are so important.

There is a statement that many people say that led me to write this book. It is, "if I knew then what I knew now, my life would be so much better." How often have you said that or heard that in your life? The older we get, the more we realize the numerous bad decisions we made. We long for an opportunity to go back in time, correct the mistakes, and reap the benefits of our better judgment in our present life. We know that this will never be the case, but what if you could learn from someone else's mistakes? Would that be beneficial to your leadership growth?

If you are like me, then the answers to those questions are "yes and yes." Because I answered yes to those questions, I sat down to write this book. As you read it, you will see that I have pulled no punches on myself or others. To be able to write freely, I have changed the names of any person who is presented in a negative light. If a person deserves a pat on the back for a job well done, I used their name.

Since most of the examples are from my time in the military, there is quite a bit of military jargon. I have worked diligently to explain as many of the terms as possible. Please do not get bogged down in the jargon, as most of it is coloring. It will not make or break the leadership lesson learned. I thank you in advance for your patience in that regard.

You may wonder why I decided to write a book on leadership. After all, the title clearly states that I am an average leader. The reason is simple. There is nothing wrong with average. Most people are ordinary; thus, I believe most people will be able to learn and develop as a leader by reading this book. The growth will come as you sit and ponder what you are reading and looking at your own life's journey. I have done this many times, from some unique places.

Sitting on a sand berm, under a full moon in Saudi Arabia, you have plenty of time to think and read. Yes, I said read.

During a desert full moon, it is so bright you can read without the need for a flashlight. I took full advantage of the full moon nights to read letters from my wife, family members, and pen-pals. I also pondered what we were doing there, what my family was doing back in the United States. I thought about how my unit got to where we were. And I thought about how my military experiences had well prepared me for the inevitable war with Iraq.

Meditating on my experiences spurred growth in my confidence. I realized my time in the 2ID in South Korea was the best possible proving ground for me. I knew no matter what our unit faced, if I remained calm and drew upon my training, my soldiers and I would be able to defeat the enemy successfully. I established as my goal to bring every soldier in my platoon home safely. I am grateful to be able to say that I accomplished that goal.

As you read this book, my goal is for you to do more than learn about how I handled different situations in my life. I want you to learn how you can take your experiences and apply the lessons learned to your life moving forward. You are a leader who wants to be the best possible version of yourself. If that were not the case, this would not be the type of book you would be reading.

I encourage you to use this book as a reference guide. Take it with you. Highlight the parts that speak to you. I can tell you that the leadership journey never ends. You will continue to learn at every level of leadership. You will continue to have setbacks at every level of leadership. The key is to use those setbacks as learning experiences. As my friend Taylor Tyson said on national television during the 2018 Miss America competition, "Every setback is a setup for your comeback."

Thank you for trusting me with your leadership growth. Enjoy the journey.

TABLE OF ABBREVIATIONS

ADAPC	Army Drug and Alcohol Prevention and Control
ADCM	Assistant Division Commander for Maneuver
AP	Assistant principals
APC	Armor Personnel Carrier
APFT	Army Physical Fitness Test
BAT	Blood alcohol test
BC	Battery Commander
CG	Commanding General
CPT	Captain
CSM	Command Sergeant Major
CTT	Common tasks training

DHG	Distinguished Honor Graduate
DLAB	Defense Language Aptitude Battery
DLI	Defense Language Institute
DLIFLS	Defense Language Institute Foreign Language School
DMG	Distinguished Military Graduates
EXEVAL	External Evaluation
FDC	Fire direction center
FSNCOIC	Fire Support Non-Commissioned Officer
FSU	Ferris State University
FTX	Field Training Exercise
GJHS	George Jenkins High School
HHC	Headquarters company
HMMWV	Highly Mobil Multi-purpose Wheeled Vehicle
IG	Inspector General
LTC	Lieutenant Colonel
MAJ	Major
MOPP	Mission Oriented Protective Posture
NCO	Non-Commissioned Officer
NCOIC	Non-Commissioned Officer in Charge
OBC	Officer Basic Course
OC	Observer controller
OCS	Officer Candidate School
OPORD	Operations Order
PAO	Public Affairs Officer
PT	Physical training
ROK	Republic of Korea
ROTC	Reserve Officer Training Corps
SFC	Sergeant First Class

SMI	Senior military instructor
SPC	Specialist
SSG	Staff Sergeant
TAC	Training Assessment Counseling

SECTION 1
LEADERS MUST—
CREATE A POSITIVE
LEADERSHIP
CLIMATE

Leadership is about making others better as a result of your presence and making sure that impact lasts in your absence.
~**Sheryl Sandberg, COO, Facebook**

1
DON'T THROW THE BAT

Take note of this: Everyone should be quick to listen, slow to speak and slow to become angry because human anger does not produce the righteousness that God desires.
~James 1:19–20

ARGUABLY, THE GREATEST closer in the history of Major League Baseball is Mariano Rivera. He had 652 saves and helped the New York Yankees win five World Series titles. However, it may be fair to add "Luckiest Man Alive" to Mariano Rivera's accolades due to my emotional outburst. You see, I was destined to be the greatest closer in the history of the major leagues, but on one fateful day, I could not control my emotions. Is that hard to believe? Well, let me tell you the rest of the story.

At the age of eleven, I was pretty sure I could be a Major League pitcher. I had amazing control, a fastball, and a changeup. Throwing strikes was not a problem for me, but getting

3

the opportunity to showcase my pitching talent was not as easy. I had to convince my Little League coach I had the goods. The season crept along, and I knew my time to pitch was waning. Finally, one day at practice, I had worn my coach down. He said, "Okay, Gregg. Let me see what you got." He squatted down and acted as my catcher. I toed the mound and looked straight at my target because no one was up to bat. I rocked back, lifted my left leg, uncoiled my body, and unleashed my fastball right down the middle.

Pop! The coach's eyes lit up. He smiled from ear to ear, threw the ball back to me, squatted down, and slapped his mitt, ready for the next pitch. I rocked back and fired another strike. He was elated, and I was overjoyed. After wowing him with my pitching ability, he told me he would put me in to pitch the next game. I'm not sure how I got home that day, but if I were a betting man, I would wager I floated on clouds.

Game day arrived, and I was very excited. Since it was my first time pitching, my coach said he did not want me to start but would put me in to pitch after the fourth inning. My coach viewed me as a closer. He depended on me to ensure our team's victory. I would be the first Mariano Rivera. Since he is four years younger, I felt confident I would beat him out as the greatest closer in Major League history. The only thing that stood between me and immortality was four innings of baseball. I put it out of my mind to get down to the business of playing baseball.

The game moved along, but our team was not doing well offensively. It seemed like the other team threw only strikes. Maybe the umpire forgot his glasses at home (at least that is what I am going with). Maybe our pitcher received the same treatment, but from an eleven-year old's perspective, it felt like the umpire was cheating for the other team.

The bottom of the fourth inning arrived, and I was coming up to bat. At the end of the inning, I would make my pitching debut, and Mariano Rivera would never even be a footnote in history. Gregg Mays' title would be "The Greatest Closer in the History of Major League Baseball."

I stepped into the batter's box, ignored the sounds of the spectators, and put pitching out of my mind. We had a ball game to win, so I wanted to focus on getting a hit. The pitcher wound up, uncoiled his body, and threw the first pitch. I steadied my bat, turned slightly to increase the torque, and I let loose with a home run swing. Boy, you should have seen the air fly right out of the park! The ball? Well, the catcher threw it back to the pitcher. The pitcher uncoiled with the next pitch, and I wasted no time unleashing my patented home run swing. Once again, the air flew out of the park, and the catcher threw the ball back to the pitcher. As the next pitch came in, it was way outside, so I let it go. When the ball hit the catcher's mitt, the umpire said, "Ball," but it sure sounded like "strike three!" I turned and looked him in the face. Yep, he *definitely* called that pitch a strike.

I thought to myself, *What? Are you blind? There is no way that was a strike! That ball was a million miles outside!* What actually happened was I looked at him, turned around, threw the bat toward the on-deck circle, and stormed toward the dugout.

As I walked to the dugout, I heard the umpire mutter something like "Hey, batter, you can't pout in this game." I was very upset and needed to calm down to be an effective pitcher at the top of the next inning. But for me, the next inning never came.

What the umpire had *actually* said to me was, "Hey, batter, you're out of the game." He tossed me from the game! The nerve of him, right? How could he throw me out of the game for almost hitting my teammate in the head with an aluminum baseball bat? I thought, *What is wrong with this guy?*

I grabbed my stuff and walked out of the dugout with my head hung low. Since my mom was in the stands, I walked over to her seat. When I got to her, she looked at me, and in her loving mom voice, said, "Oh no, you can't sit with me! I don't allow poor sports to sit with me. Walk home." So, I hung my head, walked away, and headed home. But before I got too far, I took one more look at the baseball game. One of my teammates took a third strike. He showed a little frustration, trotted back to the dugout with his head down, but he did not throw his bat. My first thought was, *Gregg, that is how you should have handled striking out.* I have never forgotten that moment in time.

In a way, Mariano Rivera should be thankful I threw my bat. He is in the Hall of Fame. Had I not thrown my bat on that fateful day, who knows?

Unfortunately for me, throwing my bat and getting tossed out of a baseball game is not the only time my emotions got the best of me. Several years later, after a mediocre college tennis career (baseball was well in my rearview mirror), I found myself playing in a doubles tournament with a young man who played for a high school team. Our opponents were okay. They were members of the country club we were playing at, but I had played against much stronger opponents during my college career. I figured we would make short work of them and move on to the next round. I was wrong.

At this stage of my athletic career, I still had not learned the importance of controlling my emotions. At one point in the match, a ball from another court rolled near the fence behind my partner and me. Our opponents were about to take a second serve when one of them called a "let," which means play must be stopped and usually comes with a restart of the point. They were to get a first serve. My partner saw the ball, picked it up, and returned it to the other court. I settled in for the second serve. When our opponent said, "First serve," I lost my cool. They called an unnecessary let when there was no interruption of the match *and* gave themselves a first serve. In reality, for them to get a first serve at that point of the game was no big deal. It was not a match point or even a set point, for that matter. To me, it was the principle that mattered. After I argued the issue for far too long, I finally dropped it. However, I did not regain my composure. I was going to show them what it felt like to play against a division one college tennis player who was, by far, the best player on the court. But a funny thing happened along the way to show them how good I was at tennis; my emotions had consumed all of my ability. I lost control. My serve was gone. Most of the shots I attempted went into the net or out of the court.

At one point, I lined up to receive a serve. When the ball came, I swung too hard. The ball hit the bottom of the net. One of the players on the other team said, "Oh, are you okay?" That infuriated me even more.

Then, it hit me. *What am I doing?* I thought. *Calm down Gregg, you're better than this.* But by the time I regained my composure, the match was too far out of reach. I had put us too deep in a hole.

Fortunately, my brother Brian was recording the match. Later, when I watched it back, I heard him say, "I'm going to make this comment now before the match is over, so it is on the video." He said, "Gregg, you're never going to be an exceptional athlete until you learn to control your emotions." He repeated it. Those words still ring clear in my head today. I use them to guide me when I want to overreact to any situation.

The final emotional misstep I want to highlight occurred while I was a company commander in the Army. Unfortunately, it took twenty-one years and a conversation with someone I worked with in that unit for me to understand that I had overreacted. When this incident happened, I felt vindicated, not wrong. My former coworker and I reconnected in Seoul, South Korea, in 2015 when I was back in the country for my in-laws' memorial service. He reminded me of the time I had called off my company's final esprit de corps run because there were not enough people present. I had retreated to my office, very upset about not having this opportunity to lead my company one last time.

For me, company runs were the highlight of our physical training program. During these runs, our unit built the camaraderie that helped spur us toward mission accomplishment. I enjoyed the different cadences our noncommissioned officers (NCOs) would call, and from time to time, they allowed me to call them as well. This was likely to be the last time in my military career that I would be able to do that during a formation; I was disappointed when it was "taken" from me. When my coworker reminded me of the incident, I could not remember it and still do not recall it. Still, I knew I was capable of such behavior at that point in my life. I said to him, "I was a child!" multiple times, I guess for effect. Our conversation was a reminder that there are consequences when you allow your feelings to take over; specifically, people remember even if you do not.

You may be asking why I started this chapter by telling a story from my childhood. Certainly, no one expects an eleven-year-old boy to master his emotions. You may also say, "It is understandable that a twenty-year-old young man would lose his cool from time to time." You may even be willing to give a thirty-one-year-old man a pass for a little outburst. Using the benefit of hindsight, I learned a very important life lesson. Every incident where my emotions got the best of me had one thing in common: I was focused on myself and how I felt. A good leader puts their focus on the mission as well as the people they are leading. If your desire is to accomplish the mission while ensuring that those whom you are leading have the best chance to excel, you must learn to set your feelings aside.

As a leader, maintaining perspective is paramount to success. The people you lead need to know that your decisions are reliable and consistent with sound judgment. They need to know that you are stable. The worst thing you can do as a leader is to "fly off the handle" when a situation seems to be out of your control. It is these times that your subordinates will look to you for direction. There is no time for a temper tantrum.

Although I still do not recall the incident where I was upset about canceling the company run, I am certain my actions were self-serving. That day, my soldiers were busier than usual. They were getting ready for my change of command ceremony. They were getting ready to have a new commander. Our company was very small, so it was easy for our physical training formation to get down to ten or fifteen people. Looking back, I wish I would have accepted that reality, but because I placed my feelings, wants, and desires ahead of the feelings of those I was leading, I had a negative reaction when things did not go how I thought they should.

As you continue to grow as a leader, take time out of your day and reflect on your decision-making. Ask yourself this very difficult question: what is my motivation for choosing this course of action? Be honest with yourself. If your honest answer is "self-gratification," then you are probably in danger of making decisions based on your emotions. Take it from me; it is not going to work out for you. Call someone you trust and respect, share your thoughts, and allow them to help you make a good, rational decision. These should be people who are not afraid to pull you aside and hold you accountable when necessary. You must have the maturity to accept and act upon constructive criticism. As a result of using this team of advisors, you will be able to make the kind of decision that everyone can live with.

When you find yourself in a situation where you have made a bad decision, learn from it, then let it go. Do not allow bad decisions to accumulate. The more you linger on it, the more negative influence it can have on your organization.

Emotions are a part of life. The key is not to use them in your decision-making process.

2
CPT CLEVER MEETS THE ADCM. TWICE

Fool me once, shame on you. Fool me twice, shame on me.
~Unknown

AS I REFLECT on the time of my first duty assignment in the Army, I am reminded of those words that brought with them the "Hallelujah" chorus. The words were "EndEx." That meant we were ending the exercise we were conducting and going back to our home station. In a unit where you were getting ready for a field exercise, conducting a field exercise, or returning from a field exercise, the latter was always the most relaxing phase. EndEx put us in that phase. For one exercise my unit completed in the winter of 1988-89, the relaxation brought on by a successful conclusion of a field exercise did not last as long as I would have liked.

Upon returning to Camp Casey from a field training exercise (FTX), our unit quickly cleaned our gear and headed out for a good meal and then back for a good night's sleep. The meal was great, but the sleep was short-lived as every unit in the Second Infantry Division (2ID) was alerted at 4:00 am the next morning. These "alerts" were called Fog-Rain exercises. It was a name used so that we knew this was an exercise as opposed to the real thing. Yes, during that era in South Korea, it was possible for the real thing to happen at any moment. Pick up a newspaper or turn on the news, and you will learn that the tension between South and North Korea is such that it is still possible, although not likely, for an actual military conflict to happen today.

I was surprised upon hearing the siren but more frustrated because our unit had come out of the field. It was always a crapshoot as to when an alert would be called. We knew they would occur at least once a month, but the exact date, we did not know. The best-case scenario is that an alert would happen while your unit was in the field. This meant that when your unit returned from the field, you were less likely to have the situation our battalion was experiencing. It should be mentioned that the Division reserved the right to have units deploy to the field for a couple of days in conjunction with a fog-rain exercise. This thought was also in my head—*Are we heading right back out to the field?*

I quickly got dressed and headed into the company. As soldiers were headed to their units, they heard over the division loudspeaker that this fog-rain exercise would be conducted in Mission Oriented Protective Posture (MOPP) Four. This meant that everyone would have on full MOPP gear—MOPP top and bottom, rubber boots, gloves, and the mask. Additionally, each unit was instructed to teach classes as a part of the exercise. The classes were to be taught in MOPP Four. Our company commander had us in the motor pool receiving these classes in the required uniform. However, because he wanted the soldiers to hear well, CPT Clever instructed the two NCO's who were teaching the class to take off their masks. This was against the orders of the commanding general (CG), a two-star general.

To ensure that everyone was complying with these orders, the CG sent out members of his staff to check on the training. One of the people he sent to check training was the assistant division commander for Maneuver (ADCM), a one-star general. To best understand what was about to happen, allow me to take you back a few days in time.

As previously mentioned, this fog-rain exercise happened on the heels of our unit returning from the field. Our unit had been on what is called an external evaluation (EXEVAL). An EXEVAL is used to assess whether or not a military unit is prepared to conduct real-world operations if the opportunity presented itself. During an EXEVAL, battalions experience multiple operational scenarios, each one different than the one before. One scenario included our battalion conducting a bridge crossing exercise. During that mission, one of the battalion's vehicles was swept downstream in a large rushing river. The vehicle was an M113 armored personnel carrier (APC), which weighed over 25,000 pounds. Fortunately, everyone was okay, but as you can imagine, the river was strong and fast. Our unit watched this incident from the shoreline. The battalion commander assessed the situation and decided that it was too dangerous to have more vehicles attempt the crossing, which meant that our company was not going to cross the river here. The seemingly good fortune we enjoyed by not conducting the river crossing in that fast-moving river was short-lived.

During our follow-on mission, our tank company inadvertently moved into a sapling-filled apple orchard. I am uncertain how long the orchard had been in place, but one thing I did know, there would be no fruit in that orchard's future with our tanks and APCs sitting on top of it.

Ruining a young orchard like that could have cost the US government millions of dollars. Farmers would be able to charge the government for lost produce. An apple orchard can take two to ten years to produce fruit, depending on how it was planted. The presence of our tank company in the middle of the orchard was bad. If we did not get out of this orchard quickly and carefully, there was about to be a very wealthy farmer.

In what would become an interesting twist of fate, the 2ID ADCM pulled up to our unit, saw what we had done, and began helping us backtrack our way out of the orchard. This was a tedious process. It was important that each track drive out on the same path on which they drove into the orchard. The ADCM showed patience as he helped ground guide several of our vehicles to safety, while CPT Clever did the same with other vehicles. Once our entire company was out, the General pulled CPT Clever aside for a discussion of the previous events. I do not know what was said, but I am sure it was something to the effect of, "Captain, you need to be careful because a mistake like this can be costly." And possibly some words that should not be printed in a book like this.

Now let us fast forward to the motor pool where we took this break in the action. You may recall that we had two NCOs teaching our soldiers, but the instructors were not wearing their masks. In the middle of one of the classes, the ADCM, yes that same ADCM, walked into the motor pool, saw the two NCOs with their masks off, and walked right over to them. He said two things, "Put your masks on immediately," and "Where is your company commander?" My first thought was, *Oh no, this is not going to turn out well for CPT Clever.* Fortunately, it did not go too poorly for him. He had a little less area on which to sit, but he got to keep his job.

As a leader, it is important to notice how much went wrong in this scenario. It would be easy to call CPT Clever out for making two poor decisions in such a short amount of time.

But that would be unfair and short-sighted. Yes, CPT Clever was the company commander and the one who was ultimately responsible for everything that went right and everything that went wrong within the company. The buck stopped with him. As a leader, this is you. The buck always starts and stops with you. If it went wrong, it is your fault. Deal with it.

But here is the thing that, as a leader, I had a problem reconciling. He did have a staff of outstanding NCOs who also had the responsibility to advise him. Additionally, he had five lieutenants who were paid to be leaders, and they, too, could have advised him better; I was one of those lieutenants. Each of us was the leader of our respective subordinate units within the company. Therefore, we were ultimately responsible for what went right or wrong within our units as well. It was not CPT Clever's place to hold our feet to the fire in this regard, but we should have held our own feet to the fire in this situation. But we did not. Why?

There are three leadership issues I want to bring to light, based on this scenario, to help me answer the why question and help you become a better leader:

1. The importance of paying attention to your surroundings.

2. The importance of speaking up.

3. The importance of creating a leadership climate in which your followers have your best interest in mind.

A statement I heard throughout my twenty-one-year military career was, "Stay alert, stay alive." If you pay attention to what is going on around you, you have a better chance of survival. CPT Clever and his leaders did not do a good job of paying attention to their surroundings. An apple orchard is easily identifiable. Regardless of the size of the trees, in this case, saplings, it looks like a farm, which is growing produce. South Korea does not have much open terrain. About every piece of land in this small country is used for something. Had CPT Clever slowed down long enough to notice, it was apparent that this open area was a farm. All of the signs were available, but he, or rather we, did not pay attention to them. As a leader, you must be aware of what is happening around you. If you are the leader of a retail business, you must know what is going on within your market. If you are a leader of a church, you must know what is going on in the lives of the members of your congregation. Being oblivious to your surroundings can be detrimental. If your goal is to be an effective leader, pay attention! Your subordinates will quickly grow weary of you saying, "I didn't know," when it is something they expect you, as the leader, to know.

When Netflix took over the video rental industry, I made the statement, "Someone at Blockbuster Video fell asleep at the wheel." I could not understand how the company with the highest market share in the video rental industry could allow another company to come along and take over the market. In his book *That Will Never Work*, Netflix co-founder Marc Randolph tells of the time the then-CEO of Blockbuster, John Antioco, appeared to be holding back laughter as Randolph and his partner made a pitch to sell Netflix to Blockbuster for $50M. Now Blockbuster is the butt of a joke. You may have heard it. A person is trying to purchase alcohol when the cashier asks for identification. Before the purchaser can pull out the ID, the cashier sees a Blockbuster Video member card on their keychain and says, "Never mind, that card tells me you're old enough." The leadership at Blockbuster was not paying attention to their surroundings. They did not under-stand that the internet market was coming, and it was not going to stop. They had the option of getting on board and riding this new train or being left at the station. If you do a Google search of Blockbuster Video, the third word in the explanation is "was." They ceased operations on September 23, 2010. As a leader, pay attention to your surroundings.

The next lesson we can learn from this is the importance of speaking up. Far too many times, I hear of people who find themselves in a bad situation who will say, "I knew this was going to happen, but I kept my mouth shut." My response is always, "Why?" If you see something, say something! I made this mistake when I was in college.

I was riding back to Tallahassee one night with a good friend of mine, Cliff Lewis. He was driving his Porsche 944 (my dream car). Far in the distance, I saw headlights coming our way. The road became winding with some construction on the road, so sometimes the two lanes became very narrow. Cliff was picking up speed and taking advantage of his car's excellent handling. All of a sudden, the car I had seen in the distance came around the corner. Cliff swerved right and then back to the left. My stomach jumped out of the car and ran alongside us for a second. Once he got the car under control, he said, "Man, that car came out of nowhere!"

I responded, "Oh no, I saw that car a few minutes ago. I thought you saw it, too."

He said, "No, I did not see it. When you see something like that, it is better to tell someone rather than to assume they see it, too. Don't keep it to yourself."

I heard that message and have lived by it ever since. People do not always like it when you say something they already know, but that does not matter; let them be upset. Had we spoken up to CPT Clever, he may have been able to stay out of both situations that led to his reprimand by the ADCM. We could have helped him avoid his second meeting with the ADCM had we insisted that our instructors not remove their masks. As a leader or a follower, when you know something is wrong, speak up. If you suspect something is about to go wrong, speak up. If you have reasonable suspicions, speak up. It is better to communicate and give your organization a chance to make an informed decision than to say nothing and suffer the consequences.

Finally, I want to discuss the importance of creating a leadership climate in which your followers have your best interest in mind. This is critical to your survival as a leader and paramount if you want to be considered an exceptional leader. Although you may be extremely good at what you do, you cannot be in multiple places at the same time. You cannot see everything your people see. Your awareness of the whole picture is minimized the bigger your organization is. Creating an environment in which people want to come to work is critical. You want them to know that their opinions matter. You want them to know that their ideas could help shape policy. Once they know this, you will have an unstoppable organization.

I am not certain if the story I am about to tell is real or myth, but the lesson is valuable. There once was a company that was befallen by difficult economic times. The leader was going to have to lay some people off to maintain the company. He sat down with the union leaders and explained the situation. The union leaders had an ingenious idea. Instead of laying people off, what if the company created a policy in which every worker had to take six weeks of unpaid leave every year. This would enable the company to save money and allow all of the workers to keep their jobs. When the union leaders explained the new policy to the workers, it was well-received. The workers began speaking to one another to organize who would take leave when and some workers, in better financial situations, even took an extra week of unpaid leave so those less fortunate would not lose money. This leader created a climate in which his people knew that they could speak to him, and he would listen. As a result, the company was saved. But, more importantly, a foundation of trust was built.

As I think about the fog-rain exercise, I wonder why we followed CPT Clever's orders to have the two NCOs take off their masks. Why had the NCOs not advised the commander that it was a bad idea? Why did I sit back in my mask and say

17

nothing? It has been too long for me to speak definitively on what the command climate was like. However, my experience tells me it is possible that CPT Clever may have created a climate in which his leaders did not have his best interest in mind. Or the NCOs did tell him taking off the masks was a bad idea, and he chose to ignore their advice. Either way, it is important for you to learn from this situation. Pay attention to your surroundings, speak up when you know something your leader may not know, and create a climate in which people have your best interest in mind.

There is one final lesson I want you to learn from CPT Clever: do the right thing no matter what. People can be upset at you because they do not like it, but your credibility will remain intact. Once you lose it, it is very difficult to get it back. By disobeying the orders of the 2ID CG, CPT Clever put himself in a bad situation as it pertained to his future orders. He set a standard that said, "If you do not agree with the orders given, change them." He did not do that on purpose, but the results of a leader blatantly disregarding the guidelines of their boss gives liberty to their subordinates when it is their turn to make the decision "to follow or not to follow."

3
THE AARON EFFECT

Sometimes you are free to your detriment.
~Bernard James (former Dallas Mavericks player)

STAFF SERGEANT AARON was my newly assigned Non-Commissioned Officer in Charge (NCOIC), whom I received while still in my first job as a second lieutenant in the US Army. He said to me, "Sir, my friends told me that if you come to South Korea an E6 and leave an E5, you had a successful tour in South Korea." He was saying that a person who only loses one pay grade while stationed in the 2ID in South Korea is successful because most people lose at least two pay grades. This was not true as most soldiers did not lose any pay grades, much less two. I thought he was joking when I heard him say that. This is not something a young officer would want to hear, especially on his first assignment within the first four months.

Almost one year after our initial meeting, I switched units, leaving D Company 1/72 armor battalion to serve in B battery

1/15 field artillery battalion. Both units were on the same Army post about one mile apart. One summer day, I was riding my bicycle toward the camp gate when I saw a soldier from the 1/72 armor battalion motor pool in the distance. He was sweeping. As I got closer, I realized it was my former NCOIC, SSG Aaron; he was now Specialist (SPC) Aaron. He did not have a successful tour.

How did he get to that place? Were there any signs of his pending fall? What could I have done to stop him from having such an unsuccessful tour in South Korea? Had I failed him, or were his initial thoughts of success in 2ID the reason for his unstoppable downward spiral? I have asked myself these questions from the time I rode past him sweeping the motor pool.

To really understand The Aaron Effect, I must provide you with some background information. Prior to SSG Aaron's arrival to the team, I had one of the best NCOs I would ultimately have in my twenty-one-year military career (I write more about SSG Widby in chapter 8, but for now, know that SSG Aaron had large shoes to fill). Because I had such an exceptional NCOIC from the beginning, I assumed that SSG Aaron was at the same level. My incorrect assumption led to what I call "The Aaron Effect."

The Aaron Effect is used to describe the multiple negative issues that arose within our team, but more specifically, what happened to him personally. The confidence of our soldiers dwindled, the credibility of our team suffered, and the productivity of SSG Aaron was non-existent. Initially, I glossed over the mistakes that SSG Aaron made, thinking they were anomalies. The problem was that he made many errors on a weekly basis. He seemed to prefer to drink coffee and shoot the breeze in lieu of training the soldiers and getting the vehicle in war-ready condition. Most good leaders would have picked up on SSG Aaron's shortcomings. Unfortunately, I did not.

I found myself training the soldiers. Any professional non-commissioned officer (NCO) reading this book at this moment will probably throw it against the nearest wall. There is no way a self-respecting NCO would have their lieutenant being the primary trainer of the unit's soldiers. When that is the case, what is the point of the NCOIC? In addition to training the soldiers, I began to find myself losing trust in SSG Aaron. I began questioning him about everything he did or did not do. In hindsight, I wonder if this reality began to shake his confidence and belief in himself as a leader.

One day while we were in the field, SSG Aaron and SPC Meeker (a soldier on our team) were having a heated discussion. I allowed it to run its course, and I discretely pulled SSG Aaron aside once they finished. I told him he could not be an effective leader if he allowed his subordinates to have a heated discussion with him in public. He loses some of his power when he does. He nodded to confirm he understood, but the damage was done. I also pulled SPC Meeker aside and told him that he was out of line. He was frustrated with SSG Aaron because he knew like I did that SSG Aaron was doing a poor job as the team's NCOIC.

I wondered at that moment if I should have stepped into the discussion sooner. Here is my leadership nugget for you: Yes, I should have stepped in and stopped it. By allowing them to conduct themselves inappropriately, I sent a message to the two other soldiers on our team that nobody was in control. Remember this: inaction is action. Fortunately, we were able to salvage the exercise and performed admirably when called upon by our higher headquarters. But the elephant was firmly in the room, and it was my job to show it the exit. I did not do my job.

Time went by, and we were preparing for the next field exercise. This particular exercise was very important as it was our unit's external evaluation where officers and NCOs from another unit evaluate your unit's ability to do its job.

A leader's reputation can be made or broken on an exercise like this. We woke up the morning of the exercise to an alert recall. Everyone was scrambling to do their job (doing it well, I might add). However, conspicuous by his absence was SSG Aaron. Our team continued working and preparing to get our vehicle ready for departure, but no one could find him. We all knew that we were leaving for the exercise on this day, so there was no excuse for him not to be there. I informed the first sergeant and the company commander that SSG Aaron was missing. The commander told me to try to find him; talk about a needle in a haystack. I got SPC Meeker, and the two of us took off on what we thought was an impossible mission. To this day, I do not remember exactly how we found him, but we did. He was at a young lady's house, drunk as I have ever seen a person. We got him to the unit, but he was in no shape to deploy with us, so he stayed in the rear.

Before we left, I pulled SPC Meeker to the side, and I said, "I need you to be the team NCOIC. Can you do it?" He looked me in the face and said, "Yes, sir!" It was a moment I will never forget. I saw so much confidence and gratitude in his eyes. He was ready and thankful for an opportunity to show that he knew his job and he could lead his fellow soldiers. It was one of the best exercises I had while in that unit. SPC Meeker performed exceptionally well. Giving him the opportunity was all that he needed. Who in your sphere of influence do you need to empower with your trust? Many times, our subordinates are waiting for us to give them an opportunity to knock our socks off, but leaders keep wearing tight socks. I am thankful that, during this storm, I was able to help a soldier experience trust in a way that could shape his career and the careers of the soldiers who would one day be under his leadership.

As the saying goes, all good things must come to an end. The exercise was over, and now it was back to reality to deal with SSG Aaron. Our crew was a company fire support team;

above us was the battalion fire support team. I went to the battalion FSNCOIC to ask for advice on how to deal with SSG Aaron, and he recommended that we pursue a field-grade Article 15, so we did. In the proceedings, I recommended that SSG Aaron receive the maximum penalty possible, which included a reduction in rank to Sgt./E5. The battalion FSNCOIC and I were asked to step out of the room before the battalion commander gave his directive. While we were out of the room, the battalion command sergeant major (CSM) recommended that we not ask to take SSG Aaron's rank, saying that if we really wanted to help him, we should recommend he be placed in the Alcohol & Drug Abuse Program (ADAPC). His logic was that we would show we really cared if we allowed him to keep his rank as long as he went through the program. He said, "If he messes up again, you can still take his rank." I thought that we should not have done this, but I had been in the unit for less than a year and had been an officer for about a year and a half. I was in no position to question the recommendation of a command sergeant major, and that is how it should be. He had far more experience than I at that point in my career. Subsequently, we accepted the command sergeant major's advice to strip him of one stripe but have the reduction deferred. This meant that as long as SSG Aaron did not get in trouble within six months of adjudicating the Article 15, he would not lose his rank. *Spoiler alert*—he got in trouble within six months!

So there I was, passing SPC Aaron as he swept the motor pool. After his second misstep, the deferred reduction in rank was reinstated, which stripped him of one stripe. He was then given another Article 15, which included the loss of another stripe. This meant that he arrived in South Korea as an E6 and was leaving as an E4.

As I pen this book, it has been about thirty-one years since this event. By the time this book goes to print and distribution, it will have been thirty-two years, if not longer. Why do

I mention this? Because that time in my life is still one of the most impactful moments of my leadership journey. I wonder what I could have done differently to possibly save this man's career. I did not mention that he was a married man when he arrived. Did my silence also cost him his career and marriage? From my perspective, no. His actions did that for him. He was capable of doing his job well; he was a functioning alcoholic. He was able to perform for a time, but maintaining that facade is difficult in the long run. The longer addicts fake it, the more destruction they cause.

As a leader, you can only influence your subordinates as much as they will let you. However, you can be consistent in your actions. You can ensure that your words and your deeds match. What is implied in this story is the reality that SSG Aaron's actions did not match his words. Most of the time, he was professional and worked well with our higher headquarters as well as with the company command structure. Our team had what we needed and was able to function, but his inconsistencies ultimately failed him; his inappropriate interaction with SPC Meeker planted a seed, and missing the field exercise planted a full-grown tree. My part in all of this is that I should have seen it coming.

You must remember that people usually do not fall from grace overnight. As the leader of the team, it is important that you keep your finger on the pulse and step in to help your team when they need it. The best leaders are able to anticipate a need and provide at a moment's notice. This inspires the team to trust the leader. As a result, your team will work harder, perform better, and do everything within their power to do right by you. That is the peak of good leadership.

Possibly the biggest lesson to take from The Aaron Effect is when things go wrong, take the time to learn every lesson you can from it, but do not stop growing. Do not convince yourself that you cannot be all that you can be. Mistakes happen, people fail, but good leaders thrive through it all.

When I left that unit, I went to the next one and had a good time there. We were able to accomplish things that other teams within our command could not. By all accounts, I had a successful second job to go along with the glowing reports from my first job in the Army. If I would have continued to kick myself for the fall of SSG Aaron, I may have had a bad career or a much shorter one.

4

DOING WHAT'S RIGHT NEVER GOES OUT OF STYLE

You always gotta do the right thing: you never know who's watching.
~John Wall

SOMEWHERE SOUTH OF the Iraqi-Saudi Arabia border, my sleep was rudely interrupted by the unmistakable sound of the M8 alarm. Unlike most alarms used by people to wake themselves up from sleeping, this alarm is an early warning system for detecting a possible chemical weapons attack. When the alarm sounds, the first thing you better do is put on all of your MOPP gear. Once that is on, then you can wake up.

I jumped out of my slumber, dawned my gear, and quickly went to the gun line. At the time, I was a platoon leader in a self-propelled artillery unit deployed in support of Operation Desert Shield/Desert Storm. I quickly arrived at the gun where the alarm had sounded and proceeded to support the section chief, who was in the process of confirming what substance was in the air, also known as the unmasking procedures. Several days earlier, an M8 alarm had triggered, but that one was a false alarm. I was inwardly praying that this one would also be a false alarm. Several minutes went by as the section chief led his soldiers through the steps toward unmasking. As they continued to work, the battery commander arrived at the gun, where I briefed him on where we were in the unmasking procedures, and we both waited for the all-clear.

The initial steps of the unmasking process focus on checking for airborne chemicals. Once the air quality tests are negative, a soldier or two are selected to unmask for a short time, then they put their masks back on and are observed for a few minutes. The soldier who is selected to take off their mask is usually the lowest ranking soldier on the gun. This is done because they are deemed to be the most expendable, which sounds harsh, but soldiers on the gun line and throughout the Army understand that role. We are taught in basic training who will be the person in the unit that will be asked to unmask, a duty not taken lightly. If no symptoms are observed, then all soldiers are directed to unmask while the NCOIC continues to observe them. As I stood next to the battery commander, the gun chief came to the unmasking step. Before the selected soldier could take off his mask, the battery commander took off his mask. This was quite a surprise. I am not certain what he hoped to accomplish by doing that, but I would later learn that some of our soldiers did not consider it to be an act of good leadership. Eventually, the all-clear was given to the unit, and everyone removed their MOPP gear and returned to their slumber.

Two things happened the next morning that have influenced me as a leader. First, the conversation I had with my platoon sergeant. He pulled me aside and said, "Sir, I was proud of you last night." I looked at him inquisitively. "When the battery commander came over here last night looking for you, I thought you were still in your rack (in bed). When he checked in there, you were already gone. At that moment, I was proud of you for taking care of your business and getting over to the gun." I gave a half-hearted thank you, but inside I was beaming. I had a great deal of respect for my platoon sergeant, so to learn that he was proud of me for something I had done was a big deal to me.

Second, the conversation I had with the gun chief whose M8 alarm malfunctioned. I walked over to his gun to see how the maintenance on his alarm was going. He pulled me aside and said, "Sir, what is wrong with the battery commander? Why did he take his mask off? Doesn't he understand that it is not his place to unmask like that? He is the battery commander; he should never do that." These were all good questions. Unfortunately, I had no good answers for him. I was not sure why the battery commander had removed his mask in lieu of allowing the selected soldier to do it. I could only speculate that he was trying to show the soldiers that he is willing to die for them, but even that is a bit of a stretch. Only one M8 alarm had triggered. If there had been an actual attack, more M8 alarms in the area would likely have triggered. That said, based on the section chief's questions, I did know one thing: the battery commander had lost some credibility among the troops. Losing credibility is never a good thing for a leader. This has been one of the most eye-opening moments of my leadership journey. I have never forgotten the disappointment the gun chief had in the battery commander, and I carried that lesson with me throughout the remainder of my military career into my time as a high school teacher today.

What is the lesson I learned? A leader must stay in their lane and do their job. It is never okay to attempt to be the hero by trying to do someone else's job. If I want to be a hero, I need to do what I can to make it easier for the team members to do their job. That is a better use of my time. That does not mean a leader cannot pitch in and do things like take out the trash, help with cleanup, or cover the phones. These things and others like them are tasks that a leader should do from time to time. But there are things that a leader should not be doing, like taking off their mask before the all-clear signal has been given.

You need to look at your area of operation and ensure that you are not stepping out of bounds in an attempt to look like a caring leader. This is a mistake that can hinder the growth of your team members. They will not be able to trust you because you will come across as someone who is trying to curry favor. Never try to make people like you. Do the right thing, and everything else will take care of itself.

The other lesson I took from this situation is related to the words my platoon sergeant spoke to me. When the M8 alarm sounded, I never thought about staying in my rack and waiting to see what was going on; my movement was immediate. For whatever reason, me doing the right thing put me in good faith through my platoon sergeant's eyes. What makes it funny is that I did not hustle because I wanted to look good; I hustled because it was the right thing to do.

In your organization, always do the right thing. There may be times when you make mistakes or fall short in your attempts to do the right thing. So what, it is going to happen. The key is to never go out of your way to do the wrong thing. I frequently tell people that I am prone to make mistakes by accident, so why would I make bad decisions on purpose? This must be your stance as well. Never take shortcuts. Never look for the easy path when you already know that is not the right thing to do.

To best ensure you are doing the right thing in the eyes of your team, talk to them. Allow them to provide feedback on the job you are doing. Something that happens in the Army is something called a "command climate" survey. This is done by the inspector general's (IG) office. The IG is provided complete access to the soldiers in a unit. Anything said to the IG is confidential; therefore, most soldiers are honest with the representative. Although your organization may not have an IG equivalent, it is in your best interest to bring someone in who can help you keep your finger on the pulse of your organization. Providing this opportunity for your team members to share their grievances without the risk of reprisal is also doing the right thing. Always keep Robin Sharma's quote on your mind: "Doing what's right never goes out of style."

SECTION 2
LEADERS MUST—
COMMUNICATE
EFFECTIVELY

The most important part of communication is
understanding.
~Dr. Dora Mays

5
THEY ONLY KNOW
WHAT YOU TELL THEM

*Be not deceived; God is not mocked: for whatsoever a man
soweth, that shall he also reap.*
~Galatians 6:7

WHEN I BECAME an officer in the Army, one of the things I
learned was that company commander was the best job for an
officer. As an artillery officer in the early stages of my career, I
was pretty good at my job and gained great experience. I did
the three main jobs a field artillery lieutenant could do: fire
support officer, fire direction officer, and a four-gun platoon
leader. These jobs were ideal for me to gain practical experience
that very few artillery lieutenants had at the time. I was a fire
support officer and fire direction officer in the 2ID located at
Camp Casey, South Korea, and I was a platoon leader during
Operations Desert Shield/Desert Storm. All signs indicated

that I was going to be an excellent field artillery battery commander. There was one problem: when I became a captain in the Army, I changed branches from field artillery to signal corps. I was very happy and thought the signal corps would be a breeze. Unfortunately, my time in the signal corps was my worst while in the Army. The good news is I did not spend that much time in the signal corps, but it was enough time for me to become the "Worst Company Commander Ever."

Before I changed branches, a field artillery major said something to me that has never left my memory. When he heard I was moving from the field artillery to the signal corps, he looked me in the eyes and said, "They eat their young." As illustrated in the previous chapter, my time as company commander revealed there was some truth to his statement.

When I was an artillery officer, it was my dream to have four lieutenants, a first sergeant, and three platoon sergeants as my primary leaders. However, the company I commanded in the signal corps was smaller than the size of a field artillery platoon, with my primary set of leaders being a second lieutenant, a first sergeant, and an operations sergeant. To say this was a bit of a letdown would be an understatement. However, these factors had nothing to do with my being the worst company commander ever. My inabilities as a company commander fell squarely on my shoulders. I had good ideas for making the command great, but I had no plan on how to implement them. I wanted soldiers to perform a certain way, but I did not put anything in place to ensure they could. So, what went wrong? My expectations were unrealistic and, most importantly, miscommunicated.

When I walked in the door of the company I was to command, I treated it as if it were a field artillery battery, but this was the signal corps. My mentality was that of a field artillery officer, but I was now leading signal corps soldiers. My job changed, not theirs. I expected them to be what they were not trained to be.

The mission of a firing platoon in a field artillery unit involves training exercises designed to acclimate soldiers to the physically demanding nature of manning firearms and explosives as well as setting up and tearing down to move on the battlefield. Soldiers can be deployed for days, weeks, or months at a time to complete their training. The field conditions are often austere, with limited access to the comforts of home. As a field artillery officer, I deployed three times for thirty days during my first nineteen months in South Korea in the 2ID. Once I transferred from South Korea to Fort Benning, GA, within two months of me arriving, our unit deployed for a little less than a month to Fort Irwin, CA. Five months after returning from Fort Irwin and several week-long field training exercises, our unit deployed to Saudi Arabia in support of Operation Desert Shield. I was more than ready to command troops in an operational/field environment.

However, our mission in the signal corps was to maintain the phone systems, computer systems, and the television signal on the post where we were located ,including the surrounding areas within our footprint. We did not have a tactical mission in the field because our equipment was stationary, so our mission did not change. When the Eighth Army conducted exercises, we continued to monitor the systems in conjunction with our normal daily mission.

When I took over command, one of the first things I wanted to do was make us look more like an "Army" unit. When the Eighth Army had a field exercise, I wanted our soldiers to be in tactical gear at all times during the day and physical training uniform at night. This attempt at making our company look like a military unit failed epically. The complaints were too numerous to count. The soldiers believed that I was unrealistic. This was a challenge for me because I had spent so much time in the field preparing for the possibility of being deployed in support of an armed conflict. I had been deployed in support of a war. I struggled with this reality in front of me in which the soldiers in my command did not feel like a tactical scenario was necessary. I sat down with my first sergeant and discussed my thoughts. He then held a meeting with the NCOs. Once they had discussed their desires with the first sergeant, all of the NCOs congregated in my office. During our discussion, I learned that the NCOs believed that my order to be tactical during the FTX was a bad idea because their training did not require them to perform in tactical gear. I accepted their request to continue business as usual through all future exercises.

My worst attribute as a company commander was that I was too wishy-washy with my decision-making. I had ideas of what our company should do for our training exercises, and I changed my mind once my reasoning was challenged. One of these challenges occurred while I was at the battalion headquarters during a training meeting. I briefed the battalion commander about our company's plan to conduct common tasks training (CTT) while road marching up one of our three mountain sites. My NCO leadership team thought the idea was good. We planned to place CTT stations along the way as we walked up the mountain. We would be able to conduct a tactical road march and complete mandatory CTT simultaneously. After the briefing, the battalion operations officer told me that she did not believe the training plan was feasible. She told me that it was not a good idea and that I should not conduct such an exercise. I was a little surprised, but she was the person MAJ Dean had told me to listen to. Because it was my company, I could have had our unit complete the training as planned, but I chose not to do it. This was a mistake on my part.

As the leader of the company, I needed to set a more consistent command climate in my decision-making. By choosing not to move forward with this training that the NCOs supported, I was making it difficult for them to predict what was going to happen. One aspect of good leadership is consistency. If the members of your team know what to expect, they can take the initiative. Since I was willing to be wishy-washy with my decision-making, I put the NCOs in a position where they were not able to be at their best. This also had a negative effect on their ability to train the soldiers in their charge.

I also made snap decisions I would later regret because I did not think them through or seek counsel. One could have cost a soldier their career. One morning, our unit was in formation, getting ready to conduct physical training. As I was standing in the formation, I smelled the stench of alcohol. I located the soldier, then had my operations NCOIC take him to the medical clinic to have a blood alcohol test drawn on him. It came back that he had an alcohol level that was in the inebriated range. I had my first sergeant create the paperwork to give the soldier a company-grade Article 15, which is a "hearing" used by commanders to punish bad behavior, specifically, behavior that is illegal or detrimental to the good order and discipline within the unit. If I could go back to that situation and do it again, I would not give the soldier an Article 15. I would have had the operations NCOIC discreetly remove the soldier from formation and allowed the NCOs to handle it the best way they knew how. By giving the NCOs this opportunity, I would have built some much-needed trust within the company.

My fifteen months in command were not good. I feel bad for my first sergeant and my operations sergeant because they had the misfortune of being there the entire time. All of my other soldiers rotated in or out during my command, so they only had to endure my lackluster command for a short time.

As I previously mentioned, I had been a pretty good artillery officer. I understood how to lead soldiers and had led them in combat. I understood the importance of good training because when the time comes to fight, you will depend on that training. If done well, it will sustain you. With all of my vast leadership experience, why was I such a bad company commander? Well, I needed a better way to communicate my expectations.

To avoid making this mistake again, I wrote my leadership philosophy and shared it with the primary leaders within my organization. My philosophy outlined my plan for the team and highlighted what was most important to me as a leader, how I expected the lines of communications to flow, and other areas that would give my team a better understanding of my intentions while we worked to accomplish our mission. Doing this for your organization will help prepare your team for your time as their leader. I cannot tell you how many leaders I speak with that do not have a mission statement. If your organization does not have one, put this book down and write one. The people who work for you are not mind-readers, so give them an idea of who you are and what is important to you. They only know what you tell them.

Additionally, as a leader, you should have a personal mission statement. It should answer five questions: who, what, when, where, and why. It does not need to answer them in that order. My personal mission statement is,

> "I will create, develop, and maintain relationships with people as I go about my normal daily activities in order to help them become better leaders as they work to achieve their personal and professional goals."

Notice that all five questions were answered in this mission statement.

> "I (who) will create, develop, and maintain relationships with people (what) as I go about my normal daily activities (where and when) in order to help them become better leaders as they work to achieve their personal and professional goals (why)."

A mission statement is simple to create, but you must put effort into it. It is not good to write something so you can have words on paper. How you live your life should be a reflection of your mission statement.

As a high school teacher, I purchase a yearbook annually. At the end of the year, when the books are distributed, I ask my students to sign mine. It is an opportunity for me to pull the book out years later and be reminded of the students I have had the pleasure to teach. The most common comment in the eleven yearbooks I currently have is, "You helped me to see that I can do anything," and "You showed me that I can do more than I thought." These comments help me to know that I am focused on my personal mission statement. My students do not know my personal mission statement, but their comments tell me that I am accomplishing the mission.

Several years after I had changed command out of that signal company, I had a dream that I was a company commander again. This time, I was so much better at leading the unit. I was more thoughtful when making decisions. I understood that I needed to assess the skills of the members of the unit and deploy these skills for the betterment of the company. I had a great time in my dream command. When I woke up, I realized I truly wanted another crack at that job. I can never go back and fix all of my mistakes, but I can learn from the biggest one I made; trying to force my company to be what it was not designed to be due to poor communication. I better understand that they only know what you tell them.

6
THE BROTHER FACTOR

The tongue has the power of life and death.
~Proverbs 18:21

I HAVE FOUR older brothers and no sisters. Three of us have had long military careers, which means our family has lived far away from one another for most of our adult lives. Starting in November 1997, my wife, daughter, and I had the opportunity to live only a few hours away from my third oldest brother, Michael. He was a career Air Force member who, like I, had been assigned to duty in California. He was stationed in Sacramento, and I was stationed at the Presidio of Monterey. I know you guys are feeling sorry for me. Trust me, it was a tough assignment, but someone had to make the sacrifice for the team.

For those of you who may not know much about the Monterey Bay area, let me tell you that some of the most breathtaking views can be seen from the shores of the Monterey

Peninsula. The famous 17 Mile Drive, Pebble Beach Golf Course, and Cannery Row are a few of the sites popular in this area. Believe me when I tell you, no one who has ever been to Monterey would feel sorry for me being "forced" to live there. My family's time in Monterey lasted until August 1999, at which time I was assigned to Seoul, South Korea.

Prior to the move, I last saw Michael on a Sunday that August when I took him to the airport for one of the far too many temporary duty assignments he had while stationed in Sacramento. It was during this ride that my brother said something that would change my life for the better. The funny thing is, I did not realize how much I longed to hear it until he said it. The belief that I have something to say in the form of a published book is directly or indirectly due to the words he spoke that day. I had no time to prepare to hear what he said, so my reaction was raw and real.

For you to better understand the significance of what he said, it is important for me to tell you a few things about my upbringing. As I mentioned, I am the youngest of five boys. All of my brothers were really good at sports or music; my brother, Brian, was good at both. Although I was respectable at sports and music, I was never as good as any of my brothers at something any two of us did. From my perspective, in this very competitive household of ours, I was, without a doubt, firmly in last place. Like many youngest siblings, my brothers teased me. One of the worst things they did was pretending to flick stuff from their noses into my food. It would gross me out and take me far too long to eat. This was especially bad when I was eating cereal with milk. It would get soggy and taste terrible (I have no problem eating soggy cereal now. Hmmm, maybe something good did come from all of that trauma).

During our childhood, I always challenged my brothers at different games and activities, but I would either lose or feel unsatisfied if I won. Winning was rare, so I did not feel unsatisfied too often. The problem was, I could not understand

41

why I felt unsatisfied. As the youngest in the family, I became consumed with doing whatever it took to stop the teasing and find some satisfaction in winning. In order to do that, I believed I needed to be better than my brothers at something, anything. So, I picked up tennis. It was slow going at first, but I kept at it, and I learned to play the game well. After hours and hours on the tennis courts, it happened: I was the best tennis player in the family. But even that did not satisfy my desire to be "better than my brothers at something, anything." I rationalized that the reason I was better than them at tennis was that I was passionate about the sport, and they were not. Beating them at tennis was not an accomplishment because we were not at the same level. I was a tennis player, and they were playing tennis.

So, there I was, a member of a very competitive family, losing at everything, feeling inadequate and dissatisfied when I did win. My behavior turned bad. I was not a good individual; however, I seemed to fake it well. Most people thought I was a nice guy, but they had no idea about the internal war that was being waged inside of me. The people who knew me had no idea how inadequate I truly felt.

Despite my negative feelings about myself, I persevered and, somehow, managed to grow up, graduate college, start a military career, marry way above myself, and have a child who is definitely in the running for the best daughter ever. And still, there was something missing. I was unable to develop a positive image of myself. The million-dollar question was, why does it seem impossible for me to find satisfaction in myself and my accomplishments? I have it all: a great wife, a great child, a great job.

For years that question lingered in the back of my mind, and sometimes, it made its way to the front. Unfortunately, I never quite understood why I could not overcome these feelings of inadequacy. I developed an inferiority complex in which I truly believed that everyone who did what I did was better at it than I. I continuously looked over my shoulder, waiting for people to pass me by in whatever it was we were doing. Trust me, that is no way to live, and it is definitely no way to be successful. Now that you have a snapshot of my childhood and life struggle let us return to the car.

As we were arriving at the airport, Michael turned and began speaking to me. He said, "Gregg, before I leave, I wanted to tell you something. Although I knew you in your childhood and teenage years as we grew up, it has been great to get to know you now, as a man." A man? My big brother called me a man! That meant the world to me. For him to see me as a man meant that he thought I was adequate. His words changed my life. When he got out of the car to catch his flight, I meditated on those words all the way back to his house. For one of my brothers to pay me such a compliment had a huge impact. I felt like my real life could start. I no longer needed to compete for respect in my family. I had it. I was adequate.

His words have propelled me to heights that I did not believe I could attain. As a man of faith, I believe that God orchestrated that moment because it was exactly what I needed to get out of the rut that I was in. I believe that God still uses these words as a reminder of His love for me. I believe that I am where I am in life because he said, "It has been great to get to know you as a man."

Having read the beginning of this chapter, you may be thinking, "Why is this chapter in a book about leadership?" Fair question. This chapter is in this book because, as a leader, it is imperative that you remember that people have baggage. They have a personal history that may have an impact on who they are and how they behave. You must always remember that you are not leading "stuff"; you are leading human beings with backgrounds.

How you interact with the people you lead can be the difference in your success or failure. When taking on a leadership role, it can be very easy to focus only on the mission of your organization. Your thoughts focused on how you and your people can be successful. On the surface, there is nothing wrong with this mentality. But if you want to be a leader that makes a difference, a leader for whom people would walk through fire on broken glass, then you must get to know them at a deeper level. You must understand that they have baggage and be willing to provide the space they need to work through their issues while still doing their job.

This will not be easy. In fact, it could be the most difficult part of being a leader. Depending on the size of your organization, you may believe that this is an uphill battle that you cannot win. When those thoughts arise, cast them down. The good news is you are reading this book. Help is in your hands.

Remember the adage that says, "People do not care how much you know until they know how much you care." As you get to know the people in your organization at an appropriate, personal level, word will spread. Your reputation as a fair and caring leader will begin to precede you. This is important because, in those moments when you believe the hill is too high, you can be reminded that you are not climbing the hill alone. You have developed a leadership atmosphere of trust. Your people will begin giving you the benefit of the doubt when you "fall short" or "do not notice a person in need of support."

The place I have seen this situation on full display is as a high school teacher. In any given classroom setting, there are over twenty-five different students with over twenty-five different backgrounds. If I want to help these students be successful, it is necessary for me to learn a little about each student. I must pay attention to their unique learning style while at the same time providing a consistent climate in which these students are able to learn and grow as young adults. In my class, students know what to expect. They also know that they are in a room with a teacher who cares about them as an individual. As we develop mutual trust, I give them space and open the door for them to tell me their story. This is always done on their timetable, not mine. As a leader, remember that; you must allow people to share their stories with you on their time, not yours.

My goal each year is to be able to provide insight into each one of my students if asked to do so. Therefore, I make sure that I do not allow my first impression of a student to be a lasting one. I have former students, too many to count, with whom I did not get along at the beginning of the school year. One year I had a student with whom I *knew* I would not get along. Fortunately, I gave her a chance, and we have an amazing relationship to this day. She even allowed me to help her choose a college. Additionally, I was able to develop a good relationship with her family.

If you want to be a leader whom everyone reveres, then you must be willing to let go of initial impressions, especially the bad ones, and let the people show you who they truly are. Better yet, help them grow into the best possible version of themselves. How can you do that? You do it by encouraging them frequently. Look for the good in people. When providing feedback, be honest, but remember that you are dealing with a person, not a thing. Sometimes being honest hurts, but this is okay when it is coming from a place of support. When possible, take their history into account. I fully understand that there are times when this is not feasible, but as a leader, you can ensure those times are rare or at least unavoidable.

Remember, sometimes the right words at the right time can unlock a person's potential and propel them to the highest of heights. Make sure you are a leader who routinely encourages their team members. You never know when the right words will come out and change a life.

7
LEAVE IT ON A HIGH NOTE

I know you think you heard what I said, but what you heard is what you think I said.
~Unkown

MY FIRST BOSS in the US Army taught me what I consider to be the most valuable lesson I learned as an Army officer. Shortly after arriving at my first unit, I was assigned to go on a field exercise as an observer controller (OC) for another unit's external evaluation. I found my seat on the bus that would take us to the camp to get our assignments when I looked up and saw CPT Wetherell standing at the front of the bus. He was not scheduled to attend this training, so his presence was a surprise. He motioned for me to come to him, so I moved quickly to the front of the bus and followed him off. He was visibly upset.

To better understand his frustration, we must go back to the beginning. But, before I take you back to the beginning, I must make it clear that I had only been in the country of South Korea for a month or two. I had never participated in an external evaluation, so it would be safe to assume that I had never planned one. Now that you are feeling compassion for me and the butt chewing I am about to get, allow me to take you back to the day I returned from the exercise planning meeting.

Upon returning, I met with the battalion fire support NCOIC to go over what I would need for the field exercise. He looked over a list of items and said, "There should be no problem for you to get all of the items on the list." Unfortunately, what I heard him say was, "There should be no problem for me to get you all of the items on the list."

The exercise was two weeks away, and I never looked at the list again. Surely you can see where this is going. Nothing was ready the morning of the movement. I assumed that the battalion NCOIC was getting everything on the list, and he was certain that I was getting them. The battalion Fire Support NCOIC had to scramble to get the items despite the fact that I had two weeks to prepare. One of the many merits of a senior NCO is the ability to make even the greenest Second Lieutenant seem like they know what they are doing. As you can tell, it had been a rather busy morning.

CPT Wetherell moved us out of sight from the people on the bus, where he began to explain to me the importance of communicating better. He helped me realize that the morning of the movement is not the time to confirm who was getting what and assured me that I would never do something like this again. He wanted me to confirm that he had made himself perfectly clear; he had. And then his entire posture changed. His eyes and body language suggested that he was no longer upset or disappointed with me. He was unexpectedly calm. He looked me in the eyes, smiled, put his hand on my shoulder, and said, "Now, go out there and do a great job like I know you can." At first, I was not sure I heard him correctly. I mean, he was the same man who had gone up one side of me and down the other. But that sentence set me on a course that I have traveled for the remainder of my life as a leader.

There is a quote that goes, "People don't care how much you know until they know how much you care." At that moment, CPT Wetherell showed me how much he cared by teaching me two valuable lessons at once. He showed me that sometimes you must make sure that a person knows they messed up. He showed me that as you ensure they understand their mistake, you do not need to embarrass them in front of others; he took me out of the sight of others. I now subscribe to the adage "praise in public and reprimand in private." People do not need to see you correcting someone's behavior unless it is time-sensitive and then only if life or limb is at risk. Any other situation can wait. Do not reprimand in public.

The second lesson CPT Wetherell taught me was to maintain my professionalism at all times. He taught me not to take things personally. If someone makes a mistake, it is not an attack on me. They made a mistake. I can let them know they made a mistake but also show I believe in them. When he put his hand on my shoulder, looked me in the eyes, and told me to go do a great job, that meant everything to me. I was set on doing my very best so that I would make CPT Wetherell proud of me.

He taught me another lesson, but I did not realize it until a few months later when CPT Wetherell was about to rotate back to the states. The other company Fire Support Officers and I took him out to dinner and drinks. As the night progressed, we found ourselves in a bar with some other soldiers, and two of them began making trouble. CPT Wetherell was prepared to do more than talk to them when I stepped in and led him outside. I told him that dealing with these guys was not worth it, that getting into a fight with these soldiers would potentially end his career. I wanted him to understand that the Army needed him as an officer to guide our lieutenants and captains. I encouraged him to think about the consequences of his actions. He calmed down, and we all went back to the camp without incident. The lesson he had taught me was that when you "chew" someone out the right way, they will have great respect for you and will be there for you when you need them to be.

Years later, I found myself in a position similar to CPT Wetherell. The military's intramural sports program encourages units to form teams for flag football, basketball, softball, soccer, and many others. Our company's basketball team was the best one in our installation. So good, we called ourselves "The Dream Team." One night while playing against another team, I was hit pretty hard, but the referee did not call a foul. On the way down the court, I noticed the refs were not watching the backcourt, so I bumped the guy (a common move in basketball). I guess he didn't get that memo because he came at me ready to fight. I grabbed him and held him until it could be broken up. We were ejected from the game. I collected my gear and left the gym.

What did I do? Here I was, the company commander for a unit, and I'm the one who got into a fight during a basketball game. As I walked around the post, gathering my thoughts, one of my NCOs came riding up on his bicycle. He said, "There you are. I've been looking all over for you." He asked if I was okay and assured me that I had not made a catastrophic mistake. He encouraged me not to worry about it and to put it out of my mind. It was difficult, but I did try to put it out of my mind, and the next day at work seemed to be business as usual.

I do not believe anyone mentioned the incident, but I apologized. It was my job to reward our soldiers when they performed well, but it was also my job to dole out the consequences for inappropriate behavior. How could I effectively do the latter part of my job if I was getting into fights during sporting events? It was the type of situation that could have created a double standard. If that had happened, it would have been difficult to regain the trust of the company. As I think about the fight on the basketball court, I realized that I learned a very valuable lesson.

After everything had settled down and I had left the gym, one of my NCOs came to find me. That may seem like a small gesture, but it is not. When you are not a good leader, people do not always bother to show that they care about you. The NCO did not have to come to find me. No one would have thought he was wrong by not finding me, but he wanted to know how I was doing to reassure me that the members of the team understood what had happened. Keep in mind, the members of the team were also members of my company. The valuable lesson I learned was that no matter how bad you think you are doing in a job, it is possible that you are the only one who thinks you are doing that poorly. It is possible that in the midst of you being the worst company commander ever, you might be positively impacting lives. That is what CPT Wetherell did for me, and his kindness reminds me to make space for humanity in leadership, even when you are setting someone straight.

People are okay with you critiquing them professionally. They are happy to learn how they can become better. The key is to understand that people want to do their job well, and they want to earn a promotion. Therefore, they are happy to receive feedback from you in order to improve their chances of getting that promotion or raise. Your professionalism inspires their professionalism.

The final lesson you should take from this phase of my leadership journey is to not take things on the job personally. CPT Wetherell was not "attacking" me personally. He was identifying a professional shortcoming. I made a mistake, and he was pointing it out for me to improve. That was his job:

to train lieutenants. If I had taken his butt chewing personally, I would have had a short and miserable military career. Remember, this all happened within a couple of months of me arriving in the unit. Fortunately, I did not take it personally. I encourage you to do the same. When your people make mistakes, keep it professional. Treat them how you would want to be treated if the situation were reversed. And when you need to provide a little backside rearrangement, end on a positive note.

8
THE LONGEST NIGHT
OF MY MILITARY
CAREER

In order to be discipled by others, a person must have a trusting heart, one that listens even when it doesn't fully comprehend or see the end result.
~Ed Townsend

ACCORDING TO DICTIONARY.COM, the definition of trust is: "To rely upon or place confidence in someone or something." As I mentioned in another chapter in this book, I spent about twenty-one years as an officer in the Army. During that time, I found myself deployed to war, stationed in South Korea several times, and stationed within NATO as well as several military facilities in the United States. As I think about some stressful times in the Army, without question, the longest night of my military career was a night I spent on Camp Casey, South Korea, about two months after I had landed on the peninsula. In order to best understand why this was such a long night, allow me to take you back a couple of months to my arrival at my first unit, D Company, 1/72 Armor battalion.

As I checked into the unit and met the other lieutenants in the company, I learned that my NCOIC was one of the best NCOs in the company. Each of the other lieutenants let me know that even though they had great NCOs, they would be more than happy to have SSG Widby as their NCOIC as well. As a new lieutenant arriving at my first unit, this music to my ears. By the time I met SSG Widby, I was excited, and he was better than advertised. His professionalism and command of the team quickly instilled confidence in me. I knew that this was going to be a great year.

A chapter in this book (The Aaron Effect) will help you understand how wrong I was. To make a long story short, SSG Widby left three months after I arrived in the country. But I digress.

The two of us quickly hit it off as a team. Our professional relationship became the envy of the other fire support teams within the battalion. As SSG Widby trained our soldiers, I joined in the training as well. He taught me about our vehicle, how to operate it, how to use the equipment in it, and how to maintain it. Everything he said, I took as gospel.

Now, let us return to the fateful night, the night that became the longest of my career. Earlier in the day, we were changing the track on our vehicle. In the 2ID, our vehicle was considered a pacing item. This meant that if anything was wrong with it, that deficiency must be fixed immediately. As SSG Widby and the soldiers were putting the track on, the other soldiers in the company began leaving for final formation and chow time. SSG Widby told the soldiers to pack it up for the night and head to formation. I paused. I guess I had a crazy look on my face because SSG Widby came over to me and said, "Sir, don't worry about this. We can put this track on in less than twenty minutes. I don't want the soldiers to miss formation and chow." I asked him what would happen if we were alerted through the night. He informed me that this was an easy thing and told me not to worry about it. Then he asked the "make it or break it" question, the one that got me right in the heart. He said, "Sir, do you trust me?"

So, there I was with the most important question hanging in the air. Do I trust him? He had given me no reason not to. This was one of those team defining moments. If I make the soldiers stay in the motor pool and fix the track, they would. But at what cost? If I allowed them to go to chow and fix the track in the morning, I would have shown that I do trust SSG Widby and would have encouraged him to reciprocate this trust with my actions. I chose the latter. But you knew that already. Otherwise, why would my night be so long?

That night while I was "sleeping," I ran what seemed like a thousand scenarios through my mind. I know I heard the alert siren at least twenty times. I met the battalion commander in the motor pool several times as he took an evening stroll to check out the vehicles. Of course, the only one he really wanted to see was mine. I woke SSG Widby up about ten times to ask him if he was sure it would only take twenty minutes to put the track on. And a host of other things I did while never leaving my bed. Finally, the sun peeked from behind the horizon. I jumped out of bed, got dressed, and headed to the first formation. I was eager to start the day and get the track back on. When I got to formation, my team was conspicuous by their absence, so I asked where they were. One of the soldiers in the headquarters platoon said, "I think they got up early and went to the motor pool." I walked quickly, but not too quickly, toward the motor pool. As I was arriving at the gate, SSG Widby and the team were walking out of the motor pool. They had already finished putting the track on. The funny thing about this is my room window was literally right next to the motor pool gate. I had not heard them go into the motor pool a few minutes earlier. Most importantly, SSG Widby was true to his word. He said they would do it in the morning and that it would not take long. I spoke nothing of my dreams through the night. I mean, did he really need to know about that?

The most important lesson I would like you to take from my long night is trusting is difficult, but it is necessary. Some of you reading this chapter might say, "You did not trust SSG Widby. You worried all night." That mindset is only half true. I *was* worried, but I did trust him. If I did not trust him, we would have stayed in the motor pool until the job was done. He said he would be able to take care of it quickly in the morning, and I left him to do that. I had the final word on this matter, and I chose to trust his judgment. My tossing and turning was not a result of not trusting SSG Widby. It was a result of my inexperience of being in the Army as well as being in this unit.

Fortunately, I had an NCO who was able to send the right messages to our soldiers. There were times when our team stayed in the motor pool long after everyone else had left. We did this for training purposes as well as vehicle maintenance. This moment was an opportunity for SSG Widby to teach our soldiers that there are times to choose to leave the motor pool with the rest of the soldiers, and there are times when you must stay late and get the job done. I am very thankful for this lesson that he taught me. I used it throughout my military career. The look in the NCOs' and the soldiers' faces when I released them from something early revealed they knew I was going to keep them longer than necessary. Each of them owed SSG Widby a debt of gratitude for showing me at the beginning of my career that anything that can be put off until tomorrow to give the team a needed break should be put off until tomorrow. This is not procrastination; this is taking care of your team.

As a leader, it is important for you to learn to show trust for your employees. More importantly, it is necessary for you to place your trust in your second in command as well as everyone in your charge. People will accomplish so much for you if you put your trust in them. If you have people whom you cannot trust, fix it or fire them. It is impossible to form a good team if trust is not the foundation. An organization in which trust is absent is an organization that will fail. The only question is, "When?"

9
SUCCESS REQUIRES PATIENCE

It's not where you start, but where you finish that counts.
~Zig Ziglar

IN AUGUST 2004, I arrived on the campus of Central Michigan University (CMU) in Mount Pleasant. I was there to be the Professor of Military Science of their Reserve Officer Training Corps (ROTC) program, which desperately needed a shot in the arm. It was rated 183 out of the 243 programs in the country. The CG in charge of Cadet Command made it clear to my boss that he was not pleased with CMU's program. This became a problem for me because the man who had donated the most money to the CMU ROTC unit let me know in clear terms that he wanted to see the program grow in numbers. His goal was for CMU to become the Texas A&M of the Midwest. Texas A&M's program is one of the largest, most well-respected ROTC units in the country. Our higher headquarters wanted us to produce a small number of higher quality lieutenants while our chief donor was more focused on getting more people into the program. This was certainly not an envious position, but I welcomed the challenge. I chose to produce quality lieutenants first then grow the program to be the Texas A&M of the Midwest.

I began developing relationships with the cadre, cadets, campus organizations, potential program donors, and the Mount Pleasant community. I learned that the former leader of the program was not well-respected by the staff and other leaders on the CMU campus, which came to benefit me. When you replace a bad leader, you will be given every opportunity to prove you are better than they were. Your team and people who knew your predecessor are rooting for you and want to help you be better. The key for me was to take some time, listen to the concerns of the staff and students who remained with the program, then use that information to make decisions.

One of the first questions I asked of my number two in charge was, "If you were in charge of the program, what is the first thing you would do?" He told me that he would want to be sent to Ferris State University (FSU) because students there could sign up for ROTC classes at FSU, but they had to come to CMU to take their classes because there was only one part-time cadre member on campus. This made it very difficult to improve the enrollment at FSU. In our discussions, I learned that there was a rich history of ROTC on campus, but the program was eventually neglected. If we could increase our enrollment over there, we would be able to boost our numbers while also improving the quality of the officer we were commissioning. I told the cadre member to research how we could get him over there, and within my first year on campus, we moved him to FSU. That move was critical to what I was trying to accomplish. I had sent the message that we are all in this together. Whatever is best for the program is what we will do. Some of our ideas worked well, some not so much. But the most important thing was that people were providing their input and knew they would be taken seriously.

Another issue that needed my immediate attention was the physical fitness program. Our unit average Army Physical Fitness Test (APFT) scores were very low. Many of the cadets feared the APFT and seemed to panic and underachieve during the tests, partially due to the threats made by my predecessor. Our staff explained that his command climate was not good, but before I could tackle the fear, I needed to assure everyone that scare tactics had no place under my leadership.

Once I learned about this fear-based command environment, what had happened the Sunday before classes started finally made sense. My first interaction with the cadets came during CMUs annual student arrival carnival held the Sunday before the first day of school. It was a time when about every organization on campus set up a booth outside of the Student Activity Center to give incoming freshmen and first-year transfer students a glance at everything that was available at CMU. The ROTC program also set up a booth. The hotel where my family and I were staying was right across the street from where the carnival was being held, so I decided to go over and experience it. I also wanted to see our cadets in action. As I walked up to the booth, I saw a young lady in an ROTC uniform on the phone. I cannot remember if I was in uniform or not, but when I walked toward her, she looked at me and hung up the phone. I asked her who was on the phone since she hung up so abruptly. She said, "It was my mom." I was shocked. I told her to please call her mother right back, that I did not want her to hang up the phone. I was walking into the area because that is where our group was. So, she called her mother back.

This was the culture of fear that I was going to have to turn around. I had a great staff, but there was one person who was truly a godsend—SFC Edgardo Ramos. He and I had been stationed together at a previous unit, and we deployed together for Operation Desert Shield/Desert Storm. He knew what type of leader I was and would be able to vouch for me until I could develop my own credibility with the staff. I could never thank him enough for his tireless support. Initially, I leaned heavily on him because I was most familiar with him. As time passed, I developed great relationships with the entire staff and was able to lean on all of them equally.

As a team, we began knocking down walls that had been built up and were keeping the organization from moving forward. The staff and the cadets worked hand-in-hand to rebuild our program into one that would be respected by Cadet Command and other departments on the CMU campus. The cadet leadership was beginning to trust that their voice was going to be heard, and it showed.

During the second semester of my first year on campus, the cadet battalion commander had an issue with something I had said or done. She came into my office to call me out for going against my word. She was clearly upset with me and the decision I had made, but she was right. I agreed with her point and apologized for not being a man of my word. I sat at my desk beaming with pride, so proud of her for standing up for her unit. She was right, and she knew it. To me, this was a pivotal moment for the program because it meant that the cadets knew from here on out that they had a voice. It would be nice to say it was all smooth sailing from that point, but that is far from the truth. We still had many walls to break down and big hills to climb.

Next up: the APFT. You may recall that one of our problems was our cadets being fearful of the APFT. We created a plan to change this narrative. Every Friday, after physical training (PT), our third-year cadets (or MS3s) would take a practice APFT. I told them not to worry about their score and that I wanted them to start thinking of the APFT as another workout. They bought into it, the scores went up, and by the time I left four years later, we had created a "300 Club" for our cadets who excelled on the APFT. Members received t-shirts that had "300 Club" on the front, and they would wear those shirts during unit PT. Our goal was for them to inspire others to attain a 300 on the APFT so they would get to wear the 300 Club PT uniform. The only stipulation to become a member was that the 300 had to come during a record APFT, not during a practice test. Eventually, we were also able to stop the "every Friday" practice APFTs as our cadets no longer feared to take the PT test.

Another problem our unit had was one that no one on our staff (including me) could fix: the enrollment numbers. We needed intervention. In the US Army, a Professor of Military Science was a position that required a lieutenant colonel, but I was a major who had been passed over for promotion. Initially, the CG did not want me in the position, but my boss went to bat for me and explained to the commander that his initial impression of me was that of a hard worker. He asked the CG to give me a chance in the position. After the first year, because our program had made great strides, he told the CG that I was the right person for the job. The CG relented and allowed me to stay in the position. I made sure that he would never regret that decision. I believe I attained that goal. By the time I left, the CMU program had risen from 183 in the country to 41.

We had a great ending, but the road to that point was rocky. There were several bad decisions made by cadre members, cadets, and myself that could have set our program back. Fortunately, they did not. Overall, our program faced adversity at several turns, but because we had become a real team, we were able to face our issues head-on and overcome every one of them.

Finally, in May 2008, the time came for me to relinquish my position as the leader of the CMU ROTC program. I had several opportunities to reflect on the job we had done as well as all that we had accomplished. I was proud to have been a part of this organization. Since it was my last as an active duty service member, I felt like I was leaving the Army on a very high note; I was not always certain that would be the case.

A few days before I was to leave, my sense of accomplishment was corroborated in the most unexpected way. I was sitting in my office at my desk when a department chair from another program in the same building came into my office. He told me that he wanted to make sure that he caught me before I left because he wanted to tell me to my face how happy he was when I arrived as the new leader for the CMU ROTC program. He said that prior to my arrival, there was an air of discontent between his organization and ours, that he and his staff did not enjoy being around us. He said that when I arrived, it was like a breath of fresh air entered the building. He said that in the beginning, he was happy to be rid of the old guy, but after working with me for a little while, he was equally happy that I was the guy in charge. I was touched by his words.

When I arrived on campus four years earlier, I did not envision any of the accolades our program received. My goal was to make little improvements one step at a time. I believed that as long as we took no steps backward, our program could survive. We did more than survive. One of our cadets earned her way into the top 100 on the annual US Army ROTC National Order of Merit list. This was a list of over four thousand cadets ranked in order from top to bottom. Being inside the top 100 meant she was in the top 3% of the nation's best ROTC cadets. We had not had a cadet attain that level in years, if ever. Unfortunately, we never became the Texas A&M of the Midwest, but we were a pretty good force to be reckoned with, and that was okay with me.

The biggest lesson I learned during my time at CMU is to have self-confidence and trust others. It would have been very easy for me to accept that I was not good enough for the job because I was not a lieutenant colonel. As a major, I had been passed over for promotion leading into my first year on the job. Ultimately, I was passed over for promotion every year I was in the position, a total of four times. Neither my branch manager, my boss, nor I could understand why I was being passed over. After the second time, I stopped thinking about it and realized the most important thing was to keep working hard to improve the program. If I had not believed in myself and my ability to do the job, our program would have suffered, or I would have been relieved of my duties. I can think of nothing worse than a leader who lacks self-confidence because it usually means insecurities are projected onto the members of the organization. Our program could not afford to have an insecure leader. Thankfully, I was not one. To be an effective leader, you must face your insecurities headfirst, gain self-confidence, and take down obstacles that stand in the way of your organization being the best it can be.

The next lesson I learned in my time at CMU was to talk and really listen to the people on my team. I have already told you about listening to the cadet battalion commander and taking the advice of my right-hand man; you may recall, we moved his daily duty location to FSU. But they were not the only people I listened to. I worked hard to be the type of leader who ensured everyone had a voice within the organization. The number of cadre members we had was small, which made it easy for me to regularly spend quality time with everyone on the team.

One day I was talking to one of the team members, and he made a comment about my willingness to overlook the wrongdoings of a certain cadre member. I asked him what he was talking about because I had no idea. He then explained an issue that had happened several weeks prior, saying that everyone else, including the cadets, knew about it, so he assumed I did as well. I did not. I will not go into detail about it because it is not the point here. My point is, if I did not try to spend quality face to face time with each team member, I could have had a major festering problem within the organization and not know anything about it. The team members thought I was looking the other way, but once I learned about it, I dealt with it swiftly. The team member who told me about the issue said, "Now I have even more respect for you than I had before. I was losing faith because I thought you knew about this and let it slide."

In the Army, we had a saying: "A leader is responsible for everything their unit does or fails to do." You are held accountable for everything that goes right or wrong in your organization, even if you know nothing about it. That is a difficult pill to swallow. It may seem unfair that you are accountable for things you are not aware of, but it does not matter. You are responsible. This means that you need to have your finger on the pulse of your team. You must create an environment of trust among your team members. They should be willing to talk to you without fear of reprisal. If my team thought that I was a "kill the messenger" type of leader, they would not have trusted me with the things I *needed* to hear. If your lines of communication are closed, it will be impossible for you to know everything that is happening within your organization. As a result, one day you may be called by your boss to explain a situation you know nothing about. Your boss will, rightly, be able to remove you from your position because you do not have a grip on what is going on with your team.

The final lesson I learned during my time at CMU was that you cannot win them all. You may recall that our chief donor wanted our program to become the Texas A&M of the Midwest, and the CG told my boss that he did not want more lieutenants from CMUs Army ROTC program; he wanted the ones we commissioned to be of good quality. With the hard work of our cadre and cadets, we were able to begin producing higher quality lieutenants, and our commissioning numbers did increase. However, at no point did we come even close to transforming into the Texas A&M of the Midwest. Our chief donor was very disappointed in me. Several times, I explained that the CG was not interested in our program becoming like Texas A&M's. I told the chief donor that once we improved the quality of the lieutenants that we were commissioning, then we could work to increase the number of cadets we had in the program. He did not seem to care what I said. No matter our accomplishments, he was not satisfied with the success of our program. As far as he was concerned, we were failing.

When it came time for me to leave the program, the chief donor had a meeting with my successor and our senior military instructor (SMI), who had been with me for about six months. During that meeting, the chief donor told my successor that I was a difficult person to work with and that he hoped he would be easier to work with. You are most likely not going to have a 100% success rate with all of your plans. People may be disappointed with your well-meaning efforts, but you must be willing to accept this reality. Leaders who have trouble reaching a particularly difficult goal run the risk of becoming too obsessed with attaining that goal. This can lead to an organization faltering in areas that would otherwise be successful with the appropriate attention. It is important to analyze the situation at every stage of your time in an organization. If your assessment shows that your plan is not realistic, change it or scrap it and make a new one. Make difficult decisions and stick to them.

I fully understand that you do not want to hear that you cannot win them all, but the sooner you accept that, the greater your success will be. Dr. Reinhold Niebuhr is credited with writing what has become known as the Serenity Prayer. It says, "God, grant me the serenity to accept the things I cannot change, courage to change the things I can, and the wisdom to know the difference." As a leader, there are times when the point of this prayer must be your calling card. Many great successful leaders have had to accept that one of their ideas was not going to work. If you want to be a great leader, you must be willing to accept this, too.

The aforementioned issue that I knew nothing about turned out to be a big deal and could have ended the military career of a cadre member. My boss wanted to give him a chance at redemption, and for a season, he became the best person we had on the team. I was so impressed with him that I sent an email to my boss glowing about how outstanding he had been. I called the cadre member into my office and showed him the email. I told him that if I was going to tell the boss about the negative, I must also tell him about the positive. Make sure that you are praising your team to your boss and let them know that you brag about their accomplishments. In this situation, the cadre member knew that he was not in our good graces, but he was working hard to fix that. I wanted to make sure that he knew his efforts were noticed and passed up the chain of command because he worked hard to rectify his lapse in judgment. I learned to give my team members a chance to redeem themselves, even when they have done the unthinkable.

Earlier in this chapter, I told you that I had been passed over for promotion to lieutenant colonel several times. After the first time, my boss contacted my branch manager and asked what was wrong with my file since the CG was on him about getting me out of the position and placing a lieutenant colonel in the position. The branch manager said that he did not understand why I had been passed over and expected me to be selected for promotion the next year; I was not. As the years went by, I no longer concerned myself with being promoted. I was more concerned about doing the best job possible. I was able to turn this hardship into an opportunity to help a colleague who was experiencing something similar.

I am a high school teacher, and in our district, we have a leadership program for educators who want to become assistant principals (AP). There was a gentleman at our high school who desperately wanted this position, so he completed the paperwork to be considered for the job and began the waiting game for selection. Each year he interviewed for jobs; each year, he was not selected. This went on for five years. After five years, if a person has not been selected for a position, they must resubmit the paperwork as if they are applying for the first time. I learned from some staff members that the guy decided to give up on becoming an assistant principal.

One day, I went to his office and told him my story. I told him that I had been passed over for promotion for four years, and no one could explain to me what kept me from being promoted. I told him that I made the decision to do my very best no matter what. I told him that I could not control whether or not I was selected for promotion, but I could control my effort. I encouraged him to resubmit his paperwork and keep doing an excellent job. He did resubmit his paperwork and was eventually selected to be an AP at another school within our district. After a few years in that job, he was selected to be the principal of his own high school. I do not know if he resubmitted his paperwork because of my story, but I do know that when you have setbacks, big or small, you must be ready to use them to help others achieve their goals.

While I was watching the 2018 Miss America Scholarship Competition, my friend Taylor Tyson, the Florida representative in the competition, was asked a question about her biggest failure. She paused, then said, "Failure is a funny word. I do not think of something as a failure. I believe that every setback is a setup for your comeback." Those words should be held in the memory of every leader. You will face setbacks. The question is, how are you going to deal with them. I chose to use mine to help others, as well as myself. What are you going to do?

SECTION 3
LEADERS MUST—BE HUMBLE

Every person that you meet knows something you don't; learn from them.

~H. Jackson Brown, Jr.

10
BAD CRITIQUES CAN BE GOOD FOR YOU

The trouble with most of us is that we'd rather be ruined by praise than saved by criticism.
~Norman Vincent Peale

IN THIS BOOK, I have written a chapter on my time as a Professor of Military Science at Central Michigan University. I purposefully left this leadership lesson out of that chapter because I believe it needs its own chapter, albeit a short one.

During my last year as the CMU ROTC leader, unbeknownst to me, I made the mistake that many people who are coming to the end of a job make: I became complacent. Before you say, "So what? Everyone does it. What's the big deal?" you must know that I was in charge of a program that commissioned officers into the United States Army. It was careless and unprofessional to give the image to cadets that I was no longer invested in their training.

In all fairness, I did not make a conscious decision to slack off. In fact, I thought I was still grinding. I did not realize that I was slacking until I received the critique sheets from my final semester as a college professor. Most of the critiques were benign, but there was one that stood out.

On the final day of the course, while students complete two critique sheets, professors leave the room so they cannot impact the opinion of the students. One part is turned in to the university, and the other is kept by the professor to read. The objective is for professors to identify their teaching weaknesses in order to make appropriate changes. I always read mine and endeavored to respond accordingly. Most of the time, the comments were generally, "You should change happy to glad" type suggestions. So, when I received this last set of critiques, I was in no rush to read them. I knew that I was no longer going to be teaching at CMU, so my focus was on preparing to out-process from the military. I was about to retire from the Army, and I had to travel to Fort Knox, Kentucky to complete my retirement paperwork. I took the critiques with me thinking I would read them when I got there as a sign of respect to the students who had taken their time to write them. I had no idea what I was going to read in one of the critiques.

I arrived at Fort Knox and began working on my retirement paperwork. Things went smoothly. Around noon the first day, we took a break, and I headed to a local restaurant for lunch. I ordered my food, took it to my table, and slid into my seat to enjoy my meal and read the critique sheets. They started out exactly as I had predicted. There were comments for growth, comments about things done well, and comments on things not done well. I enjoyed my meal as I read. I began letting my mind drift back to my retirement paperwork and the reality that in a few short hours, I was going to be out-processed from the Army after twenty-one years of serv—*Wait, what did that say?*

I stopped all other thoughts and focused on the critique I had read. A cadet had written a scathing review in response to the prompt, "What are some specific things your instructor does **that hinder or interfere with** your learning?" They said:

- Callous & Two-Faced

- Unreasonable expectations

- Unknown Expectations & Standards

- Did not adequately cover all material in Army classes

- Duty to teach was ignored

- Gave testing on unavailable materials (weapons count)

"Please give your instructor **some practical suggestions on ways to improve your learning** in this course."

- Compassion

- *Retire*

- Humility

- Give task, condition, standards

- Take suggestions

- Admit when you are wrong and/or mess up

- Never teach again

- We have other obligations other than ROTC, some more important

I was floored! I sat there for a few minutes staring at the paper. My initial thought was to throw the critique in the trash. It was so different from all of the other ones that I had ever received, not only the other ones in this envelope but *all* of the ones that I had received throughout my time as the instructor for this course. I thought this must be a disgruntled student who wanted to take their opportunity to let me have it on my way out. I sat there staring a bit more. My mind was racing. I wanted to defend myself, but then I thought, "Because I did not believe these comments accurately portrayed me as an instructor that semester does not mean that the student did not truly see me that way." If I was willing to accept the positive comments that students had made about me in the past, I had to own the unflattering comments as well. I thought, "Who am I to say that from this student's perspective, I had not displayed these attributes?" I decided to hold on to these critiques because I wanted to work hard to ensure that future comments like these could never be taken as truth.

The lesson I learned from this was that as a leader, you need to check in with your team frequently. If I had been providing a platform on which students could air their concerns throughout the semester, there might not have been a need for the student to give such a harsh critique. Open communication in all areas is critical to any organization's success.

For example, several years ago, Tom Coughlin, former head coach of the New York Giants, put together an advisory board made of twelve or so team members with whom he met regularly in order to learn what issues they had with him and the coaching staff. Prior to this group, the team struggled with communication. The players felt that Coach Coughlin was too rigid. They wanted to play hard and win a championship but also wanted to have a voice in the decision-making process. As a result of this board, directly or indirectly, the team went on to win the Super Bowl. Many sports talking heads believed that because Coughlin opened the lines of communication and let the team voice their concerns, the players were more motivated to work hard toward everyone's common goal: to win a championship.

Far too often, people wait until the boiling point before they reveal their concerns. Unfortunately, by that time, it is too late to have a rational sit-down discussion. You must ensure that the lines of communication are always open and able to flow freely in all directions. The most successful organizations communicate openly. Most importantly, be careful not to put up your defenses when less than flattering things are said about you. This could limit the desire of your team to want to continue "open" communication and can lead to problems within the organization. Problems that could be easily avoided if you recognize that you are not perfect and are willing to learn about your shortcomings so that you can correct them.

11
SUCCESS IS ITS OWN SATISFACTION

Be careful not to do your acts of righteousness before men,
to be seen by them.
~Matthew 6:1

BY FAR, THIS will be the most difficult chapter of this book for me to write. It contradicts how I want to live, but I believe it is important for me to share this aspect of leadership regardless of how I feel personally. I have started and stopped writing this chapter several times, erasing sentences and starting again. I tell you this because you are only reading the finished product, and I want you to fully understand how difficult it was for me to write this chapter. I began writing this chapter five months ago. What you read to this point is where I stopped. Even after starting and stopping, I still agonized over writing this. But thanks to a conversation with my brother, Dr. Michael Mays (The Brother Factor, chapter 6), I am much more comfortable writing this now. Enough stalling, here we go.

One of the more trying times for me as a leader happened after our unit successfully returned to the United States upon the conclusion of our deployment for Operation Desert Shield/ Desert Storm. On the day in question, I was standing at the back of our formation while several members of our battery received awards for our time in Desert Storm. I smiled, I applauded, I did everything a person does when their fellow soldiers receive recognition for a job well done. However, while I stood there watching as the awards were passed out, my mind went back to the day they were earned. As I replayed the moments leading up to these soldiers' exemplary service, I could not help but shake my head and think, "Wow, if everyone knew what really happened..." What happened? I am glad you asked. I will tell you why I was struggling standing behind that formation.

On the third day after the ground war had begun, our unit was traveling quickly across the Iraqi landscape. Our battery commander, CPT Smith, wanted to get our unit into the fight. Unfortunately, the distance we traveled required that our guns and ammunition carriers (goats) needed to stop for fuel. Once they stopped, they lost contact with our convoy. Once we realized that we did not have all of our vehicles, my driver and I turned around to get the ones we could find. We traveled into the night, eventually arriving at our final location with most of the goats, but very few of the howitzers; the goats and one howitzer were low on fuel.

The next morning, the commander of one of our sister batteries brought our missing soldiers and vehicles to our location. Now intact, our unit received a mission to support a raid on Tallil Air Base. Our commander met with the platoon leaders to go over the OPORD. I was the platoon leader for the second platoon, and as part of the execution plan, we decided that we needed to take two goats with us. I said that my platoon's goats were low on fuel and probably would not be able to make it, but if needed, I would take them. The first platoon leader volunteered two from his unit. We concluded the meeting and went back to our respective units to give the order, rehearse, and head out.

While each platoon was giving the order, our battery commander went on a route recon. The plan was that once he had completed his recon, he would contact us, and we would meet him at a predetermined location to begin the march to our firing position. We got the call and left to meet the commander, and I was the last vehicle in the route of march. Since all of the vehicles were in front of me, I immediately noticed that we had no goats with us, which meant that we only had enough ammunition to fire our planned mission one time. This was not acceptable. It left our commander and the maneuver unit's commander with no flexibility, which is never a good thing. I had my driver turn our vehicle around and go to the first platoon to get the goats, as per the plan. I asked the first NCO I saw, "Which two goats are supposed to be going with us?" He replied, "(Our platoon sergeant) told us that we are not going." I told him that this was not an option because we could not successfully complete this mission without the extra ammunition. He got his soldiers together, the other team as well, and we rolled out to catch up with the unit.

We reunited with the rest of the guns and continued to the assault position. Once we were there, the platoon sergeant from first platoon came over to me and asked why I brought the goats with us. I told him that we could not successfully complete this mission without them, but he assured me otherwise and told me that it was not my place to give his soldiers commands. I insisted we could not accomplish this mission without them, and he asked why I did not bring two from my platoon. I informed him that in our OPORD brief, his platoon leader said he would supply them. Although he did not like my answer, he seemed to resign himself to the reality that the vehicles were present, and he had to move forward from that.

As we left the assault position, I was frustrated, not understanding how someone with that much experience could not see how necessary it was for us to have extra ammunition. How could he believe that we would be at our best without a contingency plan in place? I had to put these thoughts out of my mind and shift my focus to what was happening in front of me. I was leading my soldiers into battle, and they deserved a leader with undivided attention.

We rolled into our battle position, and the gunnery sergeant and I laid and safed the platoon in a record time. To lay and safe the platoon means to put the howitzers on a specific line of fire to enable the platoon to fire with accuracy. I checked in with the fire direction center to make sure there were no needs there; then, I met with my platoon sergeant to see how the guns were. Everyone was ready. Then, the call came. Our guns were hot, and we were initiating the raid on Tallil Air Base.

Boom! Boom! Boom! The cannons fired quickly, and the sounds echoed. And then, silence. The mission was complete. Now, we were awaiting the call, "March order," which would notify us to pack up and leave our position. A call came, but it was not to march order. It was two words that changed the path of the day and left me standing at the rear of a formation, wondering what happened.

"Repeat, over!!"

Repeat! That meant that we were to fire the entire mission one more time. One of the goats had broken down, so we only had one at this point, but we *did* have one. That would be enough to provide plenty of rounds for the guns to re-fire the mission. The soldiers moved rapidly to get the necessary ammunition to fire the mission.

Boom! Boom! Boom! The cannons fired quickly, and the sounds echoed. And then, silence. Once again, we waited to hear, "March order."

"Repeat, over!!"

We fired that mission three times. Without the ammo carriers, we would have been sitting in our position with serious egg on our faces. As it was, we fired the missions as requested. Then the call finally came: "March order." Everyone breathed a sigh of relief. We had supported the raid and suffered no casualties.

That night, while sitting on the side of the road awaiting our next mission, I listened to President Bush declare that the 100-hour ground war was in a ceasefire state. Of course, I was watching and listening to weapon systems firing while he was speaking, but I did not care. I was happy. Proud, even. I knew that our unit had done a good thing that day, and I had a part in it.

Eventually, our unit redeployed to Saudi Arabia, cleaned our equipment, and loaded up for home. At no point did the first platoon sergeant ever come to me and say, "You were right." If I am honest, I really did want him to do that. He really let me have it when we were at that assault position, and I felt like he owed me that much. He did not feel the same.

So, there I was at the back of the formation, watching the platoon sergeant and his soldiers receive an award specifically for that mission. They were awarded for exemplary service in the face of battle. It was said that without the ammunition carriers, the mission would have surely failed. We were told that the first platoon leadership was to be applauded for their role in the successful completion of this mission. The battery commander received a Bronze Star for his role in the mission. Now, I will admit, he deserved his award because bringing two ammunition carriers was his idea in the first place. I stood in the back of that formation and did not say a word about my role in this mission. I guess, until now.

The most important lesson I learned from this moment in my life is, awards are not necessary for you to do things well. Although it took me some time to get to this place, I realized that getting an award for what happened that day would not have changed what happened that day. Our unit did a good job. We successfully did all that was asked of us. When we left our battle position, there was no doubt that we had been tested in battle, and we had confidence in one another to continue to fight if that was necessary. No medal on my chest was going to compare to that. I wish I had that mindset in the moment.

Subsequently, I do not view awards like I once did. Of course, it is nice to be recognized, but if you live for the recognition and awards, then you may find yourself standing at the back of a formation, frustrated when you should be back there earnestly applauding and being happy for the people who are being recognized for a job well done. There is an expression that goes, "Doing a good job is its own reward." At times, it is difficult to live by those words, but these words carry so much truth. As I think back to Desert Storm, I did a good job that day. How do I know? I watched those soldiers receive awards. Quite honestly, today, that is more than good enough for me.

I was listening to the late Jerry Clower years ago. In his stand-up routine, he said, "There is no limit to what can be accomplished if it doesn't matter who gets the credit." I played that over and over in my mind as I thought about my time in Desert Storm. As a leader, you cannot be fixated on getting credit for everything you do. At some point, you need to allow the big picture mission to override your desires. Ask yourself, *Were we successful? Did I do my part? Did I do my best?* If you can answer yes to all of those questions, that is all that matters. Let others receive the accolades and awards. You know what you have done. Let that be enough. Unless there is a monetary award, then you need to speak up for that. (hey, everything has limits)

This mentality has helped me through the years as an officer in the Army, a coach, and now as a high school teacher. You may be asking yourself, *Why is he writing about this? This contradicts what he is saying.* You would be correct; this chapter does contradict itself. But I felt it had to be written.

If you find yourself in a situation similar to mine, know that you are not alone. There are many people who must sit back and watch others receive recognition for their achievements. If you feel like this is the norm rather than the exception, then you may need to find a new place of employment. However, if it is the exception, then I encourage you to keep doing well and be mindful not to place too much emphasis on being recognized. As you maintain the right attitude, people around you will notice that you are a leader with high character. That is worth more than any award you could ever receive, monetary or otherwise. Proverbs 22:1 says, "A good name is more desirable than great riches; to be esteemed is better than silver or gold."

I have chosen to live by these words. If I receive an award, I am very grateful, but I know in my heart that I did not work hard so that I could receive that award. As a leader, you will get so much more satisfaction out of helping others achieve than you could ever get by working diligently for your own glory. When you help someone achieve, you share in their achievement. When you work for your own glory, oftentimes, you must enjoy it alone. I encourage you to seek to help others achieve; no one truly wants to celebrate alone.

SECTION 4
LEADERS MUST— PERSEVERE

Perseverance is not a long race;
it is many short races one after the other.
~**Walter Elliot (1888-1958), Scottish politician**

12
GROWTH AND GOOD TIMES

We are going through Iraq.
~Mays Family Proverb

ON AUGUST 2, 1990, Saddam Hussein, the dictator of
Iraq, ordered his army to attack the country of Kuwait. This
event had a major impact on the world, which can still be felt
today. It is amazing how one person's decision can have such a
profound and lasting effect on the lives of millions of people.
I was stationed at Fort Benning, Georgia as a platoon leader
in Alpha Battery 4/41 field artillery battalion. Our unit was
mobilized within a few days. Although I was ready to "support
and defend the Constitution against all enemies, foreign and
domestic," the timing could not have been worse.

My daughter was born on July 1, 1990, one month and
one day prior to Iraq's attack on Kuwait. Two days after the

attack, my wife and I celebrated our first wedding anniversary. Nineteen days after the attack, my unit and I boarded buses to drive to Fort Stewart, Georgia, in advance of our deployment in support of Operation Desert Shield (ODSh), which ultimately became Operation Desert Storm (ODSt). For those of you who are keeping track, you already know that we left our home station seven weeks after my daughter was born. Did I mention that the timing could not have been worse?

My initial response to being alerted for deployment was surprisingly one of calm resolve. I believe that my time as a soldier assigned to the 2ID in South Korea prepared me for this moment. The life of a soldier in the 2ID was all about field training. You were always preparing to go to the field, in the field, or had returned from the field. Being in the field means conducting field training exercises (FTX). In simpler terms, it is how Army units get ready to be successful in combat should a war ever breakout. I was in South Korea for nineteen months. Additionally, as fate would have it, for the first eleven months, I worked in two different units at the same time. I was a fire support officer assigned to an artillery battalion but further attached to an armor company. Therefore, whenever my parent unit went to the field to fire artillery rounds, the fire support teams went with them in order to train on fire observation. Whenever the armor company would go to the field to work on tactical movement, our fire support team would go with them in order to train on maneuvers. In nineteen months, I probably went to the field twenty to thirty times. The month surrounding the 1988 Summer Olympics was the only time that no units went to the field: one week before the Olympics, the two weeks of the Olympics, and one week after the Olympics had ended. This was a time that the South Korean government did not want to give the North Korean government a reason to say, "The US is committing an act of war toward our country." As a result of the hands-on experience and confidence I gained during the numerous

FTX's I conducted, at no point throughout my deployment to ODSh/ODSt did I feel overwhelmed.

On September 1, 1990, our unit arrived in Saudi Arabia. After spending a little over a week acclimating to the desert temperatures, we received our equipment and rolled to our new home somewhere in the middle of the desert. Almost immediately after our unit pushed out into the desert, rumors began to circulate of our pending redeployment back to Fort Benning, which initially stated we would be home by Halloween. When Halloween arrived, the rumor mill decided that the first report was wrong, and we would now be home by Thanksgiving. I recall having a conversation with one of our unit's medics. He was attached to our battery from a non-deploying active duty unit in the states. I said something about some training I wanted our unit to do, which was to be conducted after Thanksgiving. He looked at me and said, "Why are you planning for that? We are going to be gone by Thanksgiving." I explained to him that it would be unprofessional for me to plan our unit's training based on unsubstantiated rumors. He assured me that this was not a rumor, that his home unit had confirmed that we were heading home before Thanksgiving.

The Thanksgiving meal we ate in the desert that year was one of the best meals I have ever eaten in my life. The grapevine now said we would be home in time for Christmas! I was amazed at how seriously some of our soldiers were taking these rumors. I remember talking to one of the captains assigned to our headquarters element, and he seemed frustrated because our high command kept "changing the date of redeployment." I could not believe that a fellow officer, one with a higher rank than I, believed these rumors were true and allowed himself to be visibly and publicly emotional about it. One of my fellow lieutenants assigned to another battery took up smoking cigarettes to deal with the stress of higher headquarters constantly "changing the redeployment date." The Christmas meal was not as good as the Thanksgiving meal, but it was pretty good. In all fairness to our amazing cooks, I was brought a lukewarm-to-cold plate of food since I volunteered to pull radio watch at our platoon's area.

As we approached the new year, we developed a new attitude toward going home. Instead of seeking out and spreading the latest gossip, we encouraged the soldiers to prepare to go to war with Iraq. We let them know that the road back to Fort Benning, Georgia, went through Iraq. Once they realized the wisdom in the attitude, they stopped spreading rumors about when we were redeploying. The motto became, "Home is through Iraq."

History tells you that we did go to Iraq, where we participated in the 100-hour ground war. History tells you that we were very successful and returned to the United States to great pomp and circumstance. There were parades held in every city from which a unit deployed to the war. The citizens of Bangor, Maine, took it upon themselves to be the gateway for redeployment. They now have my utmost respect. They made it their purpose to meet and greet every plane that carried redeploying service members. We arrived in Bangor around 6:00 am, but the airport was packed as if it were noon. Kids were asking for autographs; people wanted pictures with us. The entire atmosphere was amazing. It is near the top of my list of the greatest moments of my life. My goal is to one day take my wife to Bangor, Maine, so the two of us can enjoy the city and thank the citizens for what they did at such an important time in my life. Once we were able to set gossip aside, we steeled our resolve to train well, fight hard, and bring every member of our unit home safely. To get back to Fort Benning, Georgia, we took the route through Iraq.

The primary lesson I learned during this phase of my leadership journey is that there are some difficult situations that you are going to have to experience by enduring them. This is the main one I pray that you will apply to your life. Trying to run from them is not going to work, nor is it going to benefit you as a leader. The sooner you embrace the reality that there is no way around the obstacle in front of you, the sooner you will be on your way to creating the right plan to get to the other side.

The mathematicians among you readers will have already figured out that my wife and I were married on August 4, 1989. Like most married couples, we very much enjoy celebrating this day as a reminder of the best decision we ever made. On our anniversary in 2010, my wife received a phone call from a doctor's office. However, this call did not come from her doctor but rather from the Moffitt Cancer Center located in Tampa, Florida. They asked her if she was ready to set up her appointments. My wife was confused. The person on the other end of the phone asked, "Ma'am, do you have breast cancer?"

My wife said she had never been told that by her doctors. The person said she was sorry for the call and hung up. My wife was a bit confused but thankful the lady had called the wrong number. A few minutes later, our phone rang again. This time, it was from our doctor's office. They said my wife needed to come to their office as soon as possible. When she pressed for the reason for the short notice appointment, they said they did not want to talk about it over the phone.

Well, you do not have to be Ellery Queen to figure out where this lesson is headed; my wife was diagnosed with breast cancer. What a way to spend your twenty-first wedding anniversary. However, my wife's attitude was amazing. When she told our daughter, she had a smile on her face. Our daughter was a little confused, presumably because it was odd for a person who had been diagnosed with breast cancer to have such a big smile on their face.

The "C" word was now in our household, and we had to make decisions. How were we going to move forward? A little over a month and several doctor's visits later, we sat down and had an important discussion. I explained to her what happened while I was deployed to Saudi Arabia. I shared with her that from the time we arrived in the country, rumors of our impending return to Benning spread like wildfire. I told her that in the end, we realized that the only way for us to get home was to go through Iraq. I said that we knew it was not going to be easy and that people may not come home with us. But we knew that if we wanted to go home to be with our families, the road home was through Iraq. I explained to her that together, we must adopt this mentality. She agreed.

From that moment forward, we attacked her recovery process. She was amazing. No matter what happened, we continued to say, "We are going through Iraq." This was very helpful for us. Anyone who has ever fought this disease via chemotherapy knows that there are tough days and there are better days. But if we are honest, there are no "good" days until the battle is over. Accepting that we had to go through this tough time to get to the good times provided the strength needed to persevere.

As a leader, you must also use this ideology as you prepare your team to take on the most difficult missions. It is human nature to seek an easy way around an obstacle. However, many times, taking the road less traveled right through the heart of the problem will build character within you and, subsequently, within your team members. It is a strong character that will propel you and your team to be the type of organization in which some of the best applicants want to work. I am sure you would agree that it is better to have people in your organization who want to be there, develop a strong character, and are willing to take difficult tasks head-on, knowing that growth and good times are on the other side.

Once you develop this mentality, do not lose heart. Times can get tough, outcomes can look bleak, and circumstances can consume you and wear you down. Do not allow them. When tough times come, there is no need to panic. Go through them and celebrate on the other side. We did.

13
WORK WHERE YOU'RE WANTED

Be careful of what you wish for. You might get it.
~Unknown

AS THE SAYING goes, "The grass is always greener on the other side." Of course, anyone who has chased greener pastures usually finds the other grass is just as green as the grass on their side of the fence. The reality is the grass is greener where it is watered and nurtured. Of course, this book would not be complete if there was no chapter on how I learned this lesson.

While serving in South Korea for a second time, there came a point where two viable options for company command presented themselves. In one of the units, the battalion commander wanted me. In the other unit, the battalion commander did not want me. I took the latter, which led to headaches and heartaches.

My mentor and boss at the time, MAJ Darryl Dean, came into our office one day and said a company command in a different battalion was opening. I wanted to be a company commander, so I jumped at the opportunity. As I was going through the process, our battalion commander, MAJ Dean's boss, called me into his office. He explained that he envisioned me commanding one of his companies that would be opening in several months. I understood why he wanted me to command his headquarters and headquarters company (HHC). Sometime prior to my meeting with him, I had written a memorandum. It was sternly voiced and laid out a strict policy for dealing with soldiers who had alcohol-related incidents while "out on the town." I wrote this policy in the commander's name because of a situation that I had dealt with the previous weekend. I believed that if the soldiers were held to a higher standard, there would be fewer alcohol-related problems within our battalion. Because the language left little to no wiggle room, the battalion commander did not sign the memorandum as written, but he was impressed with my willingness to take this level of initiative. Therefore, he wanted me to command his most challenging company, HHC. I was torn.

I went to MAJ Dean and asked him for advice. He suggested that I take the first job available because I did not want to appear unappreciative. Neither of us could have imagined how bad my decision would be. The new boss over the company I was to command did not want me in his unit.

You may be asking yourself how I knew I was not wanted in the company command I pursued. Well, one day, I was in my final interview with the battalion commander of the unit where I was going, and he said, "If the brigade commander (his boss) asks me which person I want, I am going to choose the other applicant." I asked him if he would prefer I remove my name from consideration, and he told me, "No." He said whoever was selected for the company command would be welcomed with open arms. I was selected for the company command, but I am still waiting for those arms to open.

During my time in command, there was a moment when I fully realized that I had made the wrong decision. Our parent unit had received a new brigade commander (my boss's new boss), and he wanted to come to visit my company's area of operation during a field exercise. In an interesting twist of fate, my former battalion commander (who wanted me to stay in his unit to command HHC) and my current battalion commander were both a part of the brigade commander's entourage during his visit. My driver and I picked up all three commanders to take them to see the different signal sites within our area of operation. While traveling to one of the sites, my former battalion commander was singing my praises to the brigade commander, a common practice of good leaders to put subordinates in good faith with the higher-ups. My new boss said nothing.

Ironically, a funny thing happened (not funny to my current battalion commander, but I chuckled to myself). We were going up a mountain to one of the sites and were now riding in two HMMWVs (Humvees) to the top. The HMMWVs belonged to another company within our battalion, not the company I commanded. I was in the trail vehicle while the brigade commander, my former boss, and my current boss were in the lead vehicle. At one point, they needed to back up in order to pass a vehicle sitting on the side of the small road we were driving on. Unfortunately, the HMMWV did not have enough clearance, and the driver broke off the side-view mirror of the vehicle that held the brigade commander *et al.* To me, this moment is steeped in irony because this would ultimately reflect poorly on my current battalion commander, who could seem to find no good thing to say about me to the brigade commander. This was in contrast to the reality that my old battalion commander shamelessly sang my praises.

In the Army, careers are made and broken by the words your leadership says about you. It is no small thing.

A few months later, I met with my battalion commander to do my mid-year review. He had some positive feedback, but I was taken aback by one of the negative comments he made. Our battalion commander had a safety policy installed to reward units for having no vehicular accidents within ninety days. He would give that unit a safety training holiday, meaning the unit could take a three-day weekend as a reward for safe driving. Within the first week or so of my command, one of our NCOs got into an accident, and since I was new in the position, the commander did not hold that against me. After that, our unit went over six months without an accident, so we received two safety training holidays. My meeting with the battalion commander was about two weeks after he signed the second safety training holiday reward. Unfortunately, after receiving the safety training holiday, one of our vehicles was involved in an accident with no injuries. Once the paperwork was finished, we moved past it. During my evaluation, the commander said he was concerned that my unit seemed to be causing too many accidents. I told him I was surprised that he would say that unsafe driving was an issue in my unit. I reminded him that we had been accident-free for over six months and that he had recently approved our second "90-day, accident-free" safety training holiday. He relented. However, the next few months were miserable. I had several conversations with our battalion chaplain to get things off my chest. Much of what occurred would be difficult to believe, even if they were written in a book. Stress became my constant companion.

Fortunately, I received a favorable evaluation report from the brigade commander (my boss's boss). I have often wondered if this was, in some small part, due to the positive words spoken by my former battalion commander. When the command was completed, I was so relieved that I went home and took a nap. I laid on the couch around noon, closed my eyes for "ten or fifteen" minutes, opened my eyes, and it was 4:00 pm. My wife told me it was the most peaceful sleep I had in the preceding fifteen months.

The lesson from this phase of my leadership journey is that the grass is always greener where it is watered and nurtured. I spent too much of my military career concerned about not making mistakes and doing what was expected of me, but this mentality hurt me during this critical time of my career. I thought if I did not take the first command offered, it meant I was not serious about taking command. I was wrong.

My former battalion commander wanted me to command a company in his unit. He would have gone to bat for me should it ever have happened, but I never gave him the chance. He told me he wanted me to command in his unit. I blew that one. As a leader, you must be able to read people. When someone is speaking truth to you, choosing to go against it is not smart. My sister-in-law, Dr. Dora Mays, has a saying: "Understanding is the most important part of communication." The battalion commanders could not have communicated their messages any clearer; one wanted me, one did not. Both of them expressed their desire to me. I encourage you to be honest with yourself and be willing to ask questions. If you are with someone with whom you cannot have an open and honest conversation, you need to start a search for a new job. Where you are has run its course. You need to be honest with yourself to ensure that you are leaving for the right reasons.

Another lesson I learned from my time in the not-much-greener pasture is to not allow outside stressors to impact your performance. While I was a company commander, I frequently allowed myself to lose focus. The command was supposed to be my number one priority at work, but it was not. This lapse in judgment also gave my boss an opportunity to find areas within my command where I fell short. As a leader, you must maintain the correct priorities. There is an adage that goes, "The main thing is to keep the main thing the main thing." I like that saying because it is a reminder that misplaced priorities are distractions that can lead to problems. When priorities are out of order, little bad things become big bad things. Remember, I was in a unit in which I was not the battalion commander's first choice, so each mistake probably became a reminder to him that he did not get his guy.

The final lesson I learned from this phase of my leadership journey is to make tough decisions, then commit to them. In this case, the tough decision would have been staying put, accepting a company command in the 307th signal battalion where the commander wanted me. The easy decision was to put my name in every hat and wait for my name to be called; that is what I did, and I paid the price. In the leadership world, what I should have done is called "taking charge of your own destiny." I did not do that. I was passive, and it cost me the opportunity to enjoy the best job an officer in the US Army will ever have.

When you are leading others, be careful not to search for greener pastures. Spend your time watering and nurturing the grass where you are. You will probably find the grass where you are is green enough for you.

14
SURVIVING BAD LEADERS

Every setback is a setup for your come back.
~Taylor Tyson, 2018 Miss Florida

WHILE I WAS serving in one of my many jobs as an Army officer, I had a conversation with one of my bosses. In her opinion, there is no such thing as a bad leader. Her contention was that if a person was a "bad leader," then they were not a leader at all. The discussion lasted for quite some time with no real resolution. She held firm to her belief while I countered that a person who leads badly is still leading; they are simply bad at it. It is safe to say that she would not approve of the title of this chapter.

In this book, I have talked about the poor leaders I have had. However, there were some things that happened during my leadership journey that needed to be said in a chapter dedicated to helping you to overcome bad leaders or at least bad decisions made by well-meaning leaders.

As the title of this book states, I am an average leader. I realize that no one is going to confuse me with Colin Powell, Tony Dungy, or Gary Brito. However, even an average leader wants their boss to listen when they are providing good recommendations. I had a boss who did not take my suggestion, and the results hurt a Non-Commissioned Officer (NCO) in our unit. This was an example of the lesson I was teaching the officer candidates in my platoon when I had them cleaning the latrine while their platoon mates exercised (the OCS latrine).

In advance of our deployment to Operation Desert Shield, our unit went to Fort Stewart, Georgia, for ten days before we shipped out to Saudi Arabia. In order to be as sharp as possible when we arrived in the country, our unit held a field training exercise (FTX). We borrowed howitzers from a local unit, drew ammunition, and headed to the firing points to send rounds downrange. Once we arrived at our firing location, one of our gun chiefs reported to me that he had been given one wrong bag of propellant; we were using white bags, but this chief was given one green bag as one of his propellants. I shared this information with the battery commander and recommended that we put the artillery round, primer, and propellant aside and turn them in at the end of the day. He said, "No, we are going to fire all of the ammunition we have." I then explained to him that this is the type of situation where an accident can happen. He said, "Make sure nothing happens."

I walked away from him and went straight to our fire direction center (FDC), where data is prepared then sent to the gun line to fire the cannons with accuracy. I explained that we had the potential for a firing mishap on one of the guns. I told them that when we get to the last fire mission that they would need to complete two sets of data—one for the white bag and one for the green bag. Once I was certain that they understood what was happening, I went to the gun chief that had the one green bag of propellant and told him to put the bag, the artillery round, and one primer to the side. I told him that when it was time for him to fire this round, he needed to confirm with the FDC that they were giving him the firing data specifically for the green bag propellant. His information was going to be different from the data that would be used for the other guns. Once I had spoken to the two major players, I went back to the battery commander. Again, I suggested that we not fire the round because, even though we are taking necessary precautions, it would still be in our best interest to return the artillery round, primer, and propellant. He said, "No."

Whether you are a leader or not, there will be times when you get an uneasy feeling that something is about to go wrong. I had that feeling. The day seemed to be going well, and soldiers were happy to be out firing rounds downrange. We had no problems, and we were coming to the end of the FTX. I went down to the gun that had the green bag propellant. I wanted to be there to make sure that nothing went wrong. While I was there, the battery commander came over to the gun and requested that I go meet with the battalion S3, who had come down to the gun line to watch us shoot. I explained what I was doing, and he said, "Don't worry about it. Our gun chiefs are professional. It will be okay." I left the gun, feeling very uneasy.

I walked over to meet the S3, and while we talked, I heard what no firing platoon leader wants to hear. "Check fire, check fire, check fire!! Rear of the piece, face the piece, fall in!" This meant that a round had not made it to the right place. Either it was short, long, or wide, but it was definitely unobserved, which meant someone could have been injured. My heart sank.

Anyone who has ever been in a field artillery unit knows that the gun chiefs are ultra-competitive with one another. The goal is to be the gun crew that gets the rounds down range first or at least gets ready to fire first. This competitive nature had reared its ugly head at the wrong time. In his haste to get his rounds down range first, the gun chief had used the wrong propellant for the data that was given to the guns. If the cannon is placed on the same data, a green bag does not send a projectile as far as a white bag. The round had fallen short. Fortunately, no one was injured, but there was going to be a stiff price to pay for this negligence. The questions to be answered were: who was negligent? and what was the price to be paid?

We did an investigation to see which gun had fired short, but I already knew what had happened. I was furious at my battery commander because he had the power to make sure that did not happen. Although he was not wrong in his decision to have us fire the round, I believed this was one of those times a leader should take the advice of those who are closer to the potential problem. That night the battery commander called me into his office and gave me a written letter of reprimand that said I had been negligent in my duties as the platoon leader, that because of my negligence, the wrong data was placed on the gun, then fired. To say that I was upset would be the understatement of the century. I was furious. I could not believe the battery commander sat there at his desk and gave me a letter saying that I was negligent in this situation. If he had listened to me and allowed us to return the munitions, this would not have happened. If he had allowed me to stay on the gun so I could be there when the last round was fired, this would not have happened. Did I say I was furious? The gun chief was relieved of duty.

I am uncertain if the battery commander had any formal responsibility, but, at the time, I felt that he should have been the guy who took the most heat. I know it seems like I was overreacting, but I told him twice that we should turn in the propellant, artillery round, and primer to guarantee that there would not have been an issue with the green bag. In addition to him not listening to my advice, he pulled me away from the gun even though I told him why I was there. I believed he should have spoken with the S3 or invited the S3 to come over to the gun to see how we maintained safety.

In Chapter 13, entitled "Work Where You Are Wanted," I talk about the battalion commander who did not want me as one of his company commanders. When he stated his preference for the other applicant, I offered to remove my name from the list of potential candidates since there were only two of us. The commander told me that whoever was selected to command the company would receive the full support of him and his staff. I was elated to be selected as the commander of 74th Signal Company. I got on the phone and spoke with the outgoing commander to work out the schedule for the change of command inventory. As a part of my discussion, I asked if it would be feasible for me to finish coaching the Area IV women's basketball team as we had earned a spot in the Korea-Wide Unit Level Basketball Tournament. Once the outgoing company commander said our change of command inventory would not be affected by my coaching, I approached the battalion commander to request permission to take the team to the tournament. He said, "Of course, you have worked hard to get to this point. You need to finish what you started." I coached the basketball team and then completed the change of command inventory quicker than we had planned.

Early in the command, my wife and I were having some marital issues —a common occurrence in military marriages. Prior to my taking command, we had planned a vacation to Japan to spend some time with my brother, Michael. Because of my new position, I was not sure we would be able to go. I had only been in the job for four months, so I felt it was too soon to go on leave. However, I was feeling the pressure at home, so I decided that I would ask. If the battalion commander declined, at least I would have asked in good faith. Fortunately, he said yes and that he understood because his wife also liked some predictability with those types of things.

Before my family and I left, our unit was having a network problem. From time to time, a circuit would break on a piece of equipment we had on a mountain site. When that happened, two of our soldiers would have to travel forty-five minutes to the top of the mountain, reset the switch, wait a few minutes to ensure that it was working properly, and then travel forty-five minutes back to the unit. Depending on what time it happened, this meant that our soldiers might have to get out of bed in the middle of the night and make this drive.

While talking to my brother, I learned it was his unit in Japan that had installed the malfunctioning equipment. When I asked my boss about going on leave, I told him I was going to have the opportunity to get information on the installation of this malfunctioning piece of equipment while I was there. I believe that was another reason that got him to say yes; he knew this was going to be a working vacation for me.

About a week after I took command, soldiers had a minor accident while driving one of our vehicles on a work call. Within our battalion, there were two companies whose soldiers did more daily driving than any other US military organization stationed on the Korean peninsula. The company I commanded was one of those units. As a safe driving incentive, the battalion commander offered a training holiday to units that went accident-free for ninety days. After that first accident, our company earned two training holidays consecutively. This meant we went one hundred and eighty days straight without incident. Shortly after earning the second training holiday, one of our soldiers had an accident.

About four or five months into my command, I received a phone call from one of the battalion's staff officers. He said, "Someone is out to get you." I was not sure what he meant, so I pressed for more information, but he said that he heard things and that I needed to make sure to do the right thing so that I would not fall short. I put the phone call out of my mind as I am not the type of person who entertains unfounded rumors. Of course, I fell short more times than I would like to admit, but I always tried to do the right thing.

Halfway through my command, I contacted the battalion commander's clerk to get on his calendar for my mid-term performance review. I arrived early on the day of the meeting. Once I was called into his office, the battalion commander and I discussed my performance. His initial comments were all positive in nature. He said that I was working hard, that he felt the unit was headed in the right direction, but he did have some concerns. I leaned in because I am a firm believer that we can grow more when we know our faults. People must be stretched in order to make the necessary changes needed to correct their deficiencies.

His first concern was that when I received the company command, I asked if I could coach the basketball team in the Korea-Wide Tournament instead of heading straight down to begin the change of command inventory. The second concern was that I asked to go on leave only four months into the command. His third concern was that my unit was having too many vehicle accidents. He said that we had four since my arrival in command. I was floored! I sat there silently at first. My mind was racing, and I wondered if I had misheard him. It did not seem possible for him to say those were his points of concern for me. I started from the top.

I said, "Sir, I asked you about the basketball tournament, and you said that you liked an officer who understood commitment. You said that it was important for me to finish what I started. And then you wished me luck." He was silent. "Additionally, sir, I explained to you about going on leave and the reality that it would be beneficial to my marriage. You told me you understood and that you, too, had to take leave in the past to keep the peace at home. When I returned from leave, I brought back the information our brigade needed to fix the problem we were having with the equipment at one of our sites." He was silent. I continued, "You said that my unit has had too many accidents. You said that we have had four since my arrival. Sir, I have only been in command for six months. You have signed the paperwork to give our unit two safety training holidays after having two ninety-day periods of accident-free driving. We have had two accidents: one when I first took command and one a few days ago, but definitely not four." Finally, I said, "Sir, I received a phone call recently. The person told me that someone here at battalion is out to get me. When I hear your areas of concern for me and my time as a commander thus far, I cannot help but believe that the person is you." (Though it worked well for me, I do not recommend that you say the last comment to your boss. It may not work in your favor.)

When the battalion commander finally spoke, he began backtracking on his comments. However, to save face, he said, "Well, two accidents are still too many," which I agreed with. I left the office concerned. If the battalion commander had it out for me, then this was going to be a very long and uncomfortable company command. It was, but in all fairness to the battalion commander, some of my issues were 100% my fault.

One of the biggest lessons I have learned from this phase of my leadership journey is how to give time a chance to teach me. You may have deduced that I was very unhappy with my firing battery commander and I felt betrayed by him. However, nothing heals wounds like time and maturity. As I have matured through the years, I look back on the situation, and I realize this: the battery commander never brought up the firing incident or the letter of reprimand again. It was almost as if it had never happened. As I began to meditate on this reality, I better understood his situation. Most likely, he had been told by his boss what he must do. He probably received zero pleasure from writing a letter of reprimand for me, and I am certain he had no pleasure in relieving the section chief. A leader must remember that things are not always as they seem.

When I was a young leader, I struggled with that. As I matured in my leadership, I was better at assessing the situation and responding accordingly. Be careful that you do not respond to a situation in such a way that you say or do something that will cause irreparable damage to your career. If you find yourself being unfairly reprimanded or worse, hold your tongue. When given the opportunity to tell your side of the story, do it with gentleness and humility. Anytime you are dealing with your boss, there is something you need to keep in mind: the boss may not always be right, but they are always the boss.

The leadership lesson I learned from my not-so-great battalion commander is that bad leaders exist. The commander was our unit's leader, and he was bad at his job. As I think back on the performance counseling, I realize that my battalion commander had a couple of options from which to choose. Prior to the meeting, he could have told me that I was doing well, but that would mean our meeting was unnecessary. I believe the better option was that he could have taken the time to do an actual assessment on me, then provide me with the feedback. I did not have a problem with him finding fault with my performance. I had a problem with what he said he found fault with because it contradicted his original words. If he had been honest with me, I would not have coached the basketball team, and I would not have taken my family to Japan. It is that simple. My "areas of concern" came as a result of me taking him at his word that it was okay for me to do those things.

While I was earning my master's degree in Ministerial Leadership, we had a discussion during one of our classes where we talked about the number one trait followers want in their leaders. According to the information used by our professor, the number one desired trait is a high moral character. Someone with high character continuously intends to do the right thing in all circumstances regardless of the potential outcome. I once had a student say to me, "Coach, you have a really good disposition. You are always doing what's right." Of course, I only wish that was true. I have definitely had lapses in judgment, but with each lesson learned, I make fewer and fewer mistakes. In my experience, my battalion commander did not display these qualities because he seemed to make decisions with self-serving interests. This is in direct contrast to a leader with high character who always keeps the interests of others in mind.

As a leader, you should seek feedback on the job you are doing. It is the best way to grow as a leader. You should ask your subordinates, peers, and superiors to give you an assessment of the job you are doing. That is what I did when I scheduled the performance review with my boss; I wanted feedback on how I was doing so that I could make the necessary changes. I was disappointed with what he said because it was inaccurate and appeared as if he had no idea how I was doing. It is not okay for a leader to have illegitimate feedback for their subordinates. When you are in charge of a team, pay attention to each member's strengths and weaknesses. Provide your assessment to them, preferably before they ask you.

When I was a basketball and tennis coach, I wrote a mid-season note to the players for several of my teams. The note addressed their performance thus far in the season. I always highlighted their strengths and an area on which they can improve. A year or so after she had left the team, one young lady shared with me that she still had the note I gave her from when she played on our tennis team. She said that it meant so much to her to get that feedback. People want to know how they are doing, but they want it to be thoughtful, authentic, and, most importantly, accurate. You are likely reading this book because you are a leader who wants more tools on their belt. Put this nugget at or near the top: the beginning of a long, lonely road to redemption is marked by the first time you are dishonest with the people in your charge. It is nearly impossible to regain trust once you lose it. Your people want to work for you. They want to do a good job for you. In return, they want to know that you are always considering their best interest when decisions are made.

15
THE OCS LATRINE

Things are not always what they seem; the first appearance deceives many.
~Plato

THE CADRE COMPANY commander's inspection began as most Officer Candidate School (OCS) inspections would: with many deficiencies identified. He was accompanied by the student company commander and student first sergeant. This was an important inspection as it signified a changing of the candidates' status where they would be promoted from basic officer candidates to intermediate officer candidates. To the outside world, this is a small thing, but to them, it meant better uniform accessories and more privileges. As a former officer candidate, I can speak from experience; you appreciate OCS privileges as if they were a priceless treasure.

As the inspection continued, things were not looking good for the company. The cadre company commander was not pleased with what he saw. The student company commander felt the beads of sweat forming on his forehead and inside his uniform. How was he going to tell the other candidates that intermediate status (along with the accompanying privileges) was going to be delayed? The student company commander was a member of the platoon I led, and I selected him because I knew he would be able to handle anything that was given to him. This time, I was wrong. He was not ready. But in his defense, no candidate would have been fully prepared for what happened next. As a matter of fact, I was not ready for what happened next. Before we continue with the inspection, please allow me to take you back to the beginning of this training cycle, back to the day that our cadre received these candidates.

My partner was an outstanding NCO named SFC Triplet, and we made a great team. We discussed our plan for the reception day and executed it better than expected. Our job was to figure out which of the platoon candidates were empowered enough to lead troops and which should return to their previous military status without completing the program. How did we do this? Lots of stress. Most handled it well, while others were invited to leave the program. One day, during our cadre company commander's morning briefing, we learned that we were going to have an extra two hours with the candidates due to a scheduling conflict with one of the post's training units. We were going to have to occupy the time of the candidates for two hours, which we had not previously planned. I told SFC Triplet that I had an idea.

When the time came, I went up to our platoon area and walked into the latrine for inspection. I stepped out into the hall and asked for the student platoon sergeant to identify the squad in charge of cleaning the latrine. I had the squad join me on my inspection. Once I pointed out the deficiencies, we returned to the hall where the rest of the platoon was standing beside their respective room doors at the position of attention. I made them get down and do push-ups while the squad cleaned.

When doing push-ups was too tiring, I had the platoon switch to flutter kicks. The exercise session continued, rotating from push-ups to flutter kicks and back until the squad leader told me the latrine was ready for inspection. It did not pass. So, the squad cleaned while the platoon exercised.

At one point, I had a couple of the squad members walk with me in the hall, looking at their platoon mates sweat. I told them to look at their faces and remember that these candidates had done nothing wrong. I explained to them that as a leader, sometimes you do not feel the burden of your mistakes, but your soldiers do. After a while, I gave the platoon a water break sending them to their respective rooms. I also told them to take that opportunity to cuss me out but to do it at a low volume so I would not hear it. They returned shortly back to the exercise session while the squad feverishly cleaned the latrine.

Finally, after about an hour and a half, the latrine passed inspection. It was immaculate! Every area of that latrine was practically perfect. The exhaust fan was spotless, the shower stalls impeccable. Sinks, mirrors, pedestals—check, check, check. I told the platoon that this was the standard when the unit was not actively using the latrine. This standard applied to every area for which our platoon was responsible, including the common areas.

Now that you are caught up to speed let us return to the cadre company commander's inspection. You may recall that it was not going well. The student company commander had recorded several of the deficiencies identified by the cadre company commander. Finally, the inspection found its way to our platoon area. He seemed to be pleased. Then, he walked into the latrine. He looked around and sent the student company commander to call every candidate to do a walkthrough. After everyone had seen it, he told the student company commander, "Now *this* is an OCS latrine!" The student company commander was beaming with pride for himself and his fellow platoon members. All of their hard work had paid off in the most unlikely of ways; the cadre company commander actually admitted that something met OCS standards. Our platoon was shocked. No one was prepared to hear the cadre company commander make such a positive proclamation.

To put this into perspective, the cadre company commander literally gave his Army career up to be at OCS. He was an officer candidate, then came back to OCS after his officer basic course, where he worked as a lieutenant, got promoted to captain, and finally became a company commander of an OCS company. Unfortunately, he spent so much time at OCS that he became an at-risk officer for non-promotion because he had almost no experience in his career branch. In the Army, a branch is the specialty area in which you work, like Infantry, Field Artillery, signal corps, Transportation, and others. His lack of Transportation experience was magnified because it occurred during the time when the Army was in a major drawdown. People were offered early retirement packages while others were given the opportunity to separate from the Army and receive severance pay, but no long-term benefits. The cadre company commander chose the latter. Before he left the Army and completed his command at OCS, he lived, ate, drank, and breathed OCS. For him to give a compliment of that magnitude was unheard of. Our platoon members were proud of themselves. SFC Triplet and I were proud of them. The student company commander could barely contain himself as he told us what happened. Heck, even I had to take a seat when I heard that the cadre company commander had made such a compliment.

They did attain intermediate status, continued through the course, and after four weeks, the candidates were ready for senior status. However, moving up came with another inspection. This time the senior Training Assessment Counseling (TAC) officer conducted the inspection. If the platoon passed inspection, they were allowed to begin their weekend pass away from the unit. Those who did not pass had to correct their deficiencies before they could begin their weekend pass. Only our platoon passed inspection the first time. You may recall, I said that the standard did not stop at the latrine. If our platoon was responsible, then excellence was the only acceptable standard.

I received a phone call from the candidates asking to borrow the boom box they saw in my office. When I walked into the building to get it for them, I noticed that everyone else was still in uniform except the members of our platoon. They told me what had happened with the senior TAC's inspection. They shared with me that at the beginning of the course, other platoons felt sorry for them. They were happy not to be in our platoon. As our platoon members walked past them headed out to Columbus, Georgia, to have fun in civilian clothes, the tune of the other candidates had changed. Now they said how much they wished they were in our platoon. Finally, the candidates in our platoon seemed to understand why we had been so hard on them. They certainly were grateful for the standard SFC Triplet and I had set because they were now reaping the benefits of maintaining these high standards.

As a leader, you must set high standards, and then you must be consistent in maintaining them. My ability to enforce the standard at OCS the way that I did is unique to that environment. You are not going to be able to have your organization's members exercising while the standard is met, but you must enforce the standards appropriately. It is essential that you *do not compromise*. A leader who sets a high standard and is uncompromising about it can be successful in short order. There will be times when people will doubt you, especially those whom you are leading. They will want to rebel, possibly calling your standards unrealistic or unattainable, but do not waiver if you know it is possible. The members of your team may get upset as you take them to new heights, but they will not complain when they get to the top and receive recognition for their hard work.

One thing that I did not mention about my time at OCS was the requirement I gave to my candidates regarding morning hygiene. From the time the morning physical training (PT) formation was released, they had ten minutes to get upstairs to the platoon area, in and out of the showers, dressed, and begin their morning chores. They were the only platoon in the company who had that requirement and it applied to me as well. Of course, I had an unfair advantage; I had a shower in my office, and I could be in my office much quicker than they could get upstairs to the platoon area. Why did I do this? Time management. I knew that if I did not push the platoon to be done with hygiene quickly, some of them would take their time and leave all of the work to the ones who moved quickly. The time restraint ensured everyone was there at the same time. The day they attained senior status, I went upstairs immediately after PT and told the student platoon sergeant that they could take their time doing their morning hygiene. The word spread quickly, and they were elated. When your team attains the standard, let them know. Allow them to celebrate this accomplishment. If you have set a tough standard, they should be excited about reaching it. A celebration makes sense.

As a high school teacher, I continuously tell my students that the standard does not come down. If they want to do well in the class, they must rise to the standard. Some accept the challenge, while others want to give up. My goal is to focus on the ones who do not give up while continuing to encourage the ones who do. Wanting to give up is not permanent. You can push them, but whatever you do, *do not lower the standard*. If the bar is set at the bare minimum, there is no incentive to do better and be better.

I once overheard a student say something to another student that let me know I was doing the right thing. She said she did not like me at the beginning of the school year, but as time passed, she began to appreciate what I was doing. She said, "Coach Mays is the first teacher who made me think for myself; no other teacher has done that." When I heard that, I jumped for joy inside. Ironically enough, that young lady's name is Joy. As a leader, you should aim to challenge your team with the intention for them to overcome obstacles and achieve their goals. People want to be challenged and stretched. If you have set a challenging but attainable standard, your team members will work hard to accomplish it.

Oh, and to finish this chapter right, please indulge me as I brag on the candidates. I told you that our company commander had informed us that we had an additional two hours with the candidates. I also told you that the TAC NCO agreed to my plan, which was to get the latrine cleaned at a very high level so that the candidates would only have to maintain it moving forward. This meant that they would not have to work so hard for the big inspections. The plan was designed to make their lives easier in the long run. I never shared this with the candidates, so for all they knew, our time together was for me to give them a smoke break since we had some extra time. A "smoke break" is the term used when you are making your soldiers work extra hard doing exercises.

At the end of each cycle, the candidates take an end of course APFT. The highest score for the test is supposed to be 300; however, if a person scores 100 points in each of the three events, they can receive extra points in each area depending on their raw score in each category. Our platoon APFT average was 296. Ten of our candidates scored at least 300, several others in the 297-299 range, and only one person was below 290. He scored 280, a very respectable APFT score considering that was the top average in the entire company.

At the end of each cycle, the company selects a Distinguished Honor Graduate (DHG) and the Distinguished Military Graduates (DMG). These are very difficult honors to achieve as there is a competitive review board that the candidates must attend. Only one person is chosen for DHG, and spots for DMGs are very limited. Our platoon members claimed the DHG award, and three others were recognized with DMG status, a very notable achievement considering the circumstances. To say SFC Triplet and I were proud of their accomplishments would be a gross understatement. The candidates bought into what we were doing, begrudgingly at first, but ultimately, they began to excel in all areas of the course because they were used to a high level of stress.

As a leader, you must be intentional. Have a plan for getting to the standard, then diligently execute that plan. Again, make sure your plan is appropriate for your work environment. Our platoon's success was dependent on our ability to create, vet, and execute the plan to its fullest.

16
THE ONE WITH THE COPY MACHINES

Do the right thing and remain consistent in it.
~Dr. Gregg Mays

ONE OF THE most interesting times of my military career was the short tour I did at the Defense Language Institute Foreign Language School (DLIFLS, aka DLI). Prior to my time at DLI, I was assigned to the Republic of Korea (ROK) Army College where South Korean Army majors attended to receive their staff officer training, the entirety of which was taught in the Korean language. It was very challenging, but prior to attending the ROK Army College, I completed a Korean language school. The timing of my assignment to DLI could not have been better.

After a stressful two years in South Korea, I was stationed at the Presidio of Monterey in California, and I was very excited about this new adventure. The first school I worked at was called European School II, where students learned Russian as well as Persian Farsi. Since I had no experience with either language, I was happy to learn that my job was going to be that of the facilities manager. I had a staff of about four people plus a daily "supply" of soldiers, sailors, airmen, and marines detailed to our school for an honest day's work. I settled into the job well ,and I loved it. My boss was an Air Force lieutenant colonel whom I enjoyed working for because he allowed me to do my job without excess overwatch. He gave me his intent along with his requirements, and off I went.

As time went on, we had two issues that needed my attention: the general cleanliness of our building and the copy machines. We had a cleaning crew who took care of the bathrooms, floors, and things of that nature, but our problem was how the rooms looked when class was in session and students were present. It looked more like an undisciplined high school student's bedroom than a building in which professional military members learned. This was unacceptable. If we were to have one visit from a high ranking official, several leaders in the building (myself included) would be called on the carpet to explain this unkempt facility. Since it was my responsibility to ensure our building was up to military standards at all times, I began implementing policies to facilitate this makeover.

I walked through the building, making note of any deficiencies, then reported them to the school NCOIC. It was his job to instruct the military members to fix them. Each day I would arrive at the school early in the morning or stay late at night to walk the entire building alone. If I saw trash, I would pick it up and bring it to the NCOIC's office so he would see it when he came to work in the morning and knew he needed to see me. After a week or so, I walked into his office one day and asked him to follow me. He looked a bit put off, but he got up, and we began walking the building. As we walked, I asked him to look in every room and notice the overall cleanliness of the building. As we finished our walk, he was smiling from ear to ear.

I told him, "Now, since we have this as our standard, we never need to tell our students to do anything special in the event we may have distinguished visitors to come without warning." He told me he was frustrated with my approach at first, but the results were worth it. As satisfying as it was to see my persistence pay off in the maintenance of the building, the copy machine issue required every ounce of patience and diplomacy with which God has blessed me.

One day while chairing a meeting, the Dean of European School II announced that there needed to be better accountability with the copy machines in the building. He was very specific about which machines could be used for what type of copies. I took note of his instructions then set about to ensure that our school followed them. I meticulously monitored the use of all of the copy machines keeping track of every copy and where it came from. Once I had an idea of which machines needed to be where I changed the location of the copy machines in order to maximize the usage. Initially, the new program was met with much resistance, but everyone soon fell in line.

About two months or so into this process, we had another meeting. The dean of the school stood up and said, "Before we get started, I want to take an opportunity to recognize CPT Mays for his efforts with our copy machines. I have returned from a dean's meeting in which every school on campus has been told they are losing copy machines. Every school except one: our school." Immediately, the room erupted in applause and joyous laughter. He and several department heads went on to thank me for sticking to my plan despite their frustration in the beginning. I needed to stand firm in the execution of my plan in order for us to keep all the copy machines we had in our school.

The common thread of these two stories is persistence. As a leader, you are going to face opposition, but it is important that you remain focused on the objective. The goal for the cleanliness of the building was to ensure that we did not need to make a big fuss in order to be ready for distinguished visitors. This sends a very clear message; the standard is the standard. Far too often, leaders allow the standard to slip, so when it comes time for an inspection, everyone has to work extra to pass. I believe in developing and maintaining the highest standard so that you never need to do anything special when your bosses are coming to visit. Will they push back? Yes. But your people will appreciate not having to put in the extra time ahead of inspections and visitors. This will be because you did your job well by enforcing the standard at all times.

I once said, "People do not like change, but they do not like things the way they are." When it came to the copy machines, I knew what needed to be done, and I had the organization's best interest in mind when I set out to implement the plan. I saw and understood the bigger picture. The department chairs were focused on their department needs, but it was important for them to make sure that the instructors in their department had what they needed. Subsequently, I implemented a plan that enabled our school to maintain 100% of our copy machines. Expect to be met with resistance. If you know you have a clear vision and you are going in the right direction, stick to your plan, and it will pay off.

Probably the greatest benefit to my persistence is the trust I gained from all who were involved. The NCOIC gained trust in me once he knew that I was willing to be a part of the solution and not point my fingers. The department chairs trusted me when they realized that if I did not intervene, our school would have lost its assets. Finally, my boss gained trust in me because he knew he could give me his intent and push me out the door. As a leader, established trust and persistence between you and your employees will take you far.

17
MAKE CLEAR GOALS, THEN CHASE THEM

Luck is the residue of hard work and design.
~Branch Rickey

WHILE I WAS attending the Field Artillery Officer Basic Course (OBC), I saw a short story on *60 Minutes*, *20/20*, or one of those news magazine shows where they talked about the military's DLI/FLS located at the Presidio of Monterey in Monterey, California. I thought to myself, *I want to go there.* So, I set that as one of my career goals to go to DLI/FLS.

Within a few days, I went to see CPT Schmills, who was in charge of the members of my OBC class. His job was to help us with our future assignments and any administrative issues we might have, so I asked him what it would take for me to be able to go to DLI/FLS in Monterey. He said because I was a field artillery officer, it would probably never happen.

I told him that I understood but that I still wanted to know the steps. He said I needed to take the Defense Language Aptitude Battery (DLAB). Although he was very reluctant, he made an appointment for me to take it.

A little background on the DLAB: it is not a test that has any actual languages as a part of the assessment. There is a made-up language to tests one's ability to learn languages, and your score on the test dictates what language you may be asked to study. The scores range from the eighties to well over one hundred; I scored a 112. I mention this because it will be important later in this chapter. For now, know that a 112 is pretty good.

Over the next five years, I married Son Hui, who was born and raised in South Korea. We had our daughter, Candice Michele, and I was on my second assignment in South Korea. At some point during this assignment, the Army sent me paperwork and asked me to choose my secondary branch. A branch in the Army is the type of job you do. For example, I was a field artillery officer when I started my career, but by the time I received this paperwork, I was in the signal corps. You may be familiar with infantry, armor, aviation, etc. Secondary branches are the ones most people know very little about. These are branches for somewhat obscure jobs in the Army. One option was public affairs officer (PAO). Since my original major in college was journalism, I selected PAO. However, when I received the letter informing me of my new secondary branch, it was not PAO, but rather FAO, foreign area officer.

The Army wanted me to learn Korean, which is considered a difficult language to learn. Why did they want me to study that particular language? Because I had scored a 112 on the DLAB, which I had taken about five years earlier. Only those individuals who score above a 100 are allowed to study languages the military deems difficult. And where do you think I was going to learn the Korean language? If you said DLI/FLS, you would be—

Wrong!

I was bummed. My branch specialty was 48H, meaning my primary area of the world was Northeast Asia, specifically South Korea. We were selected to learn the language in South Korea at Sogang University as a part of two years of "in-country" training. I spent thirteen months of my two years at Sogang. I enjoyed it, but it was not my dream of going to Monterey, California.

So, right about now, you may be asking, "Gregg, why do you have me reading this chapter?" Well, after my two years of in-country training, which also included seven months at the ROK Army College, I was stationed in Monterey. Trust me, being a cadre member in Monterey was much better than my time would have been if I were there learning the language. I know this because one of my jobs, while I was stationed at DLI/FLS, was as the associate dean of the Korean language school. Those students did not look like they were having as much fun learning the Korean language as I had learning at Sogang University.

Of course, you may have guessed that I did go to Monterey since I talk about my time at DLI/FLS located at the Presidio of Monterey in a previous chapter. But, you have to admit, the suspense was good, right?

I know this is a very short chapter, but I pray you understand it is important. The lesson I want you to extract from this phase of my life is to prepare yourself for a chance to achieve the goals you have set for your life. Time is the one commodity that we all have the exact same amount of—twenty-four hours per day. How you use your time will separate you from others.

Some people talk about what they want, but they do not take the steps necessary for them to get the thing that they want. I knew I wanted to go to Monterey, and I knew that taking the DLAB would put me in the best position to get there, so I took the DLAB. Once I took it, that was all I could do at the time, so I did not spend any time concerning myself about getting to Monterey. From the time I took the DLAB until the time I was stationed at DLI/FLS, about ten years passed. I never gave up on my desire to go to Monterey, but I also never allowed myself to be consumed by this desire. I did all I could do then I allowed life to play out. Once I was stationed in Monterey, I spent about twenty-one months there, which was long enough; Monterey is expensive.

The other lesson I want you to take from this chapter is to not allow someone else's beliefs to interfere with your plan. When you are in the preparation phase of your dreams, you must maintain your focus. The smallest, most insignificant thing can be the difference in you achieving your goal.

No one should want you to reach your life goals more than you. If someone wants you to attain your goals more than you, then *stop* what you are doing!!! You are not pursuing a life that *you* truly want. It should not be possible for someone else to want something more than you want it for yourself; there is not enough time in the day for that level of poor time management. Use your precious time to pursue life goals that you desperately want, life goals that no one else could ever want you to accomplish more than you want to achieve them. This is what I have done with the time allotted to me. And this is why I have been able to realize many of my life goals.

The next goal on my list: write a book about practical leadership. I hope I can do it!

ABOUT THE AUTHOR

Gregg Mays is a lifelong public servant-leader. He spent twenty-one years as an officer in the US Army, retired, and began a second career as a high school teacher. He is the founder of Agape Leaders, a ministry that seeks to help churches and organizations develop leaders who can better share the gospel. He holds a Doctor of Ministry in Pastoral Leadership from Andersonville Theological Seminary and a Masters of Ministerial Leadership from Southeastern University. He specializes in leadership development. During his time in the military, he trained soldiers to become officers. He did this while assigned to the US Army Officer Candidate School at Fort Benning, Georgia, and to the ROTC at Central Michigan University, Mount Pleasant, Michigan. In addition to his military leadership experience, Gregg has extensive leadership experience in sports. He coached basketball and tennis for over thirty years at varying levels to include high school varsity, college club teams, and garrison level military teams. He understands how to develop and maintain a positive team climate. He also was a character coach for football programs at Central Michigan University and George Jenkins High School, Lakeland, Florida. In this role, he gave spiritually focused chapel talks weekly. He also has given chapel talks to the football teams at the University of Cincinnati, Eastern Michigan University, and Eastern Kentucky University, among others. As a ministry leader, Gregg has experience at starting youth ministries from the ground up, as well as sustaining established programs. He has been a leader in churches around the world, including time as an elder for two different churches.

Gregg is an active volunteer for the Miss Florida Organization, which is a part of the Miss America Organization. This program provides a platform for young women to develop as leaders. His experiences include helping plan and execute the 2019 and 2020 Miss Lakeland competitions and judging four competitions: the 2018 Miss Florida Outstanding Teen competition, the 2019 Miss Pasco County competition, the 2019 Miss St. Petersburg competition, and the 2020 Miss Florida Citrus/Miss Winter Haven competition.

With his experience in the military, coaching, leading church ministries, and the Miss Florida Organization, he has gained the knowledge necessary to provide practical leadership advice to today's up and coming leaders.

Gregg has been married for thirty-one years to his wife, Son Hui. They have one daughter, Michele Jang, an actress with credits including *Life of the Party*, *Black Lightning*, and *Brockmire*. Gregg and Son Hui live in Lakeland, Florida, where he is a high school teacher at George Jenkins High School (GJHS), and she is a para-educator at GJHS. They actively attend The Rock Community Church.

Gregg frequently gets the opportunity to speak at churches, schools, and other organizations in the central Florida area to share the gospel or conduct leadership development workshops.

Contact Gregg at greggmays@agapeleaders.org or via the Agape Leaders website www.agapeleaders.org to book him for your leadership development needs.

Checkout Word Wednesday weekly on the Agape Leaders Facebook and Instagram pages, as well as on the YouTube channel. Search Gregg Mays greggmays@agapeleaders.org.

Other Agape Leaders content includes Monday Motivation (YouTube channel) and the Agape Letters (Agape Leaders website).

agape
LEADERS

OUR PILLARS

CANDOR

COMPETENCE

COMMITMENT

CHARACTER

GROW
YOUR
FAITH
EVERY WEDNESDAY
word
WEDNESDAY
with Dr. Gregg Mays
DIRECTOR, AGAPE LEADERS

ENCOURAGING
+
ENLIGHTENING
+
FOCUSED
=

motivation
MONDAY

sponsored by
agape
LEADERS

GUYNN FAMILY
PRODUCE

THANK YOU
FOR SPONSORING THIS BOOK!

CPSIA information can be obtained
at www.ICGtesting.com
Printed in the USA
BVHW040436190421
R12132700001B/R121327PG604148BVX00001B/1/J